Smart Land Management and Planning Interventions

Smart Land Management and Planning Interventions

Learning from South Korea's half-century experiences

First edition published by Seoul National University Press in 2021

Seoul National University Press
1 Gwanak-ro, Gwanak-gu, Seoul 08826, Republic of Korea
Tel: +82-2-880-5252
Fax: +82-2-889-0785
Homepage: http://www.snupress.com
Facebook: @snupress1947
Instagram: @snupress
E-mail: snubook@snu.ac.kr

ISBN 978-89-521-3051-8 (93980)

This work was supported by the National Research Foundation of Korea (NRF) grant funded by the Korea government (MSIT) (2020R1A2C4002751).

Smart Land Management and Planning Interventions

Learning from South Korea's half-century experiences

Saehoon Kim et al.

SNUPRESS
Seoul National University Press

| Contents |

Tables

Figures

Case studies

Interviews

SUMMARY

During the first half of the twentieth century, cities and rural areas in the Korean peninsula were substantially damaged. The Japanese occupation of Korea – which began in 1910 and ended at the end of World War II in 1945 – and the intermediary period of the U.S. military government rule after the liberation, followed by the Korean War (1950–1953), left a devastating legacy. Traumatized by political chaos and social instability, a large number of Koreans returned home to find their land occupied by a variety of tenants and refugees.

Development challenges such as post-war damage, homelessness, overcrowding, and food scarcity emerged due to rapid urbanization. In cities like Seoul, for example, the population tripled from 2.4 million in 1960 to 8.4 million in 1980 with an inflow of rural-to-urban migrants, return-of-war refugees, and the rise of the baby-boomer generation. The spread of illegal settlements, unemployment, inherited poverty, and land tenure insecurity often disturbed the livelihoods of urban citizens. In non-urban areas, reforming the uneven ownership of farmlands – which were formerly owned by Japanese landholdings and absentee landlords – and protecting biodiversity sites from uncontrolled sprawling became emerging issues.

This study attempts to identify a set of policies and planning actions implemented in the country's fragile condition in the aftermath of a devastating war. The focus is on land-related policies and spatial approaches that guided the growth of South Korea. Despite ongoing questions on sustainability, the country's economy and society recovered quickly from the slump. The estimated per-capita income was approximately $100 in 1963; this grew to $6,600 in 1990 and then doubled to $14,000 in 2004; urban slums were replaced with modern apartment blocks; opportunities for quality education had widened. From an urban planning perspective, integration of national territorial plans, city master plans, and urban renewal proposals presented a coordinated vision for change.

This was partially due to the secured access to land for efficient uses, the governments' timely intervention in the conflicts between landowners and *de facto* occupants, the rapid action on the spread of illegal settlements, and the establishment of legal frameworks for generating tax revenue from land. Undoubtedly, the process has been far from smooth. Policy emphasis was not always on equitable distribution and encountered resistance from residents and temporary occupants. Nonetheless, few argue against the belief that South Korea moved swiftly from an impoverished, third-world nation at the forefront of the Cold War to a model of dynamic growth. Secured land ownership and effective landuse practices enabled the manifestation of the country's comparative advantage in educated labor, competent firms, and strategic positioning in the global market.

In this study, the following actions or policies were identified to be attributable to the sustained growth of South Korea. First, the registration and management of land-related information were prioritized from the early days. This included registering the land, assessing the value, documenting changes in ownerships, and intervening in the conflicts of unclear property rights. Since the first-of-a-kind land survey took place in the 1910s, land registration maps that covered the entire nation were developed, providing a legal binding force on both landowners and local authorities. This entitled numerous benefits. For example, documents of registered lands provided a basis for conflict resolution on land boundaries, decisions on compensation for the loss of land, and administrative restraint on illegal use of land by individuals. In addition, registration and legal entitlements were important in terms of protecting individuals' property rights and restricting disapproved use of land underlying the growth of democratic capitalism in South Korea.

Second, the governments took the initiative to promote land development for the benefits of the public while attempting to reduce the negative social impacts. By 1956, only 2.7 million housing units remained habitable in South Korea, whereas over 3.8 million housing units were estimated to be required to accommodate the national population. Facing the degradation of the right to housing, public authorities took a series of actions to resolve the issue of the housing shortage. The removal of shantytowns in the city center was initiated, followed by the relocation of the occupants; publicly financed housing complexes were built; public institutions such as national-level housing corporations and local-level urban development corporations were established for rapid actions. Social inclusion was occasionally compromised, thereby leading to the marginalization of the affected people. Throughout the late 1970s and early 80s, the governments moved forward to serve as a legal implementer for large-scale land development. The responsibility involved securing new land, compensating the former landowners, and providing a master plan for approval and basic infrastructure. Although strained in certain cases, the basic legitimacy of government intervention in housing remained intact over time.

Third, the unevenness of land ownership and imbalanced gain from land transactions was addressed based on public policies, which led to mixed results. For example, rural lands in the early 1950s were predominantly owned by a few landlords. They hired tenant farmers – constituting approximately 77.7 percent of the Korean farmers in 1942 – who produced crops from labor but remained poor and mired in debt, with no means to invest. To provide the impoverished farmers with rightful access to land, the Farmland Reform Act was enacted to redistribute land to those people who were willing to live in a rural area and cultivate their own lands. The landlords were mandated to sell their farmlands, which were acquired by the government through land-value bills. Then, the lands were re-sold to self-cultivating farmers at a reasonable price. Although resisted by landlords, restructuring the agricultural land was one of the triggers of progressing from feudalism to a democratic market economy in a nation with scarce land and stagnated farm yields. In addition, policies on land taxation were implemented, and reporting the use of land for the acquisition was mandated to resolve the uneven ownership of land properties.

Fourth, forested areas and farmlands in the periphery of major cities were designated the green belt for protection. By 1977, an area of 5,397 square kilometers, or 5.4 percent of the national territory, were included in the green belt. Beginning in the early 1970s, a variety of development activities were strictly controlled within the belt. The effort was largely respected by the citizens, but generated both costs and dissatisfaction. A critical issue was that the military regime that had national security concerns designated the space by simply zoning them and maintained them afterward, without acquiring the lands. Thus, the property rights of the private landowners were often neglected, whereas the local governments had to assume the administrative responsibility of managing both the lands in the green belt and civil complaints from the occupants regarding land uses. The push and pull of policymakers, landowners, and unlicensed users in the green belt are still in progress.

What can be learned from these experiences? First, the establishment of a legal basis for owning, using, and expropriating the land was very important. Based on this, managing land registries transparently and potential land disputes equitably could build a mutually reliable foundation between the public and the private sectors. This is important to other developing countries where customary use of land can threaten the safety net of marginalized families and small business owners. Second, streamlining land administration and geospatial information can help to effectively implement land policies. Policy practices such as land readjustment, new town development, and restoration of a stream require a clear direction for intervention and investment. To achieve this, land administration services like assessing land value, responding to civil complaints, and investigating records of land transactions must be coordinated with appropriate, up-to-date technology. Third, the utilization of geospatial information must be incorporated not only in land management and dispute resolution, but also in job creation, support for vulnerable populations, and capacity-building of public officials. In fact, geospatial analysis provides a valuable tool to optimize the deployment of limited human resources and financing for multiple purposes.

ACKNOWLEDGMENTS

The conduct of the research took the form of a research group seminar in Urban Studies and Design Lab at Seoul National University Graduate School of Environmental Studies. The seminar was open to an external researcher and six Ph.D. students from the lab during the Spring semester of 2020. They were: Jihun Mun, Gukhwa Jang, Sehyung Won, Ph.D., Young Eun Kim, Hayoung Kim, Kyung-in Choi, and So Young Lee. They co-authored all of the contents in the book. The initial manuscript was reviewed and edited by Sea Eun Cho, Ph.D., and the final editing work was supported by the National Research Foundation of Korea (NRF) grant funded by the Korea government (MSIT, 2020R1A2C4002751).

Saehoon Kim, Dr.
Associate Professor of Urban Studies and Design
Seoul National University Graduate School of Environmental Studies

Chapter 1

INTRODUCTION

Growth is associated with numerous benefits. Industrial growth leads to an increase in the number of jobs, which generates wealth for the state and individuals. A wealthier nation is capable of providing opportunities for better education and other social infrastructure, thereby helping citizens to be prepared for a better future. However, the downside of growth-oriented development can be energy abuse, environmental problems, and social inequality. In a society of intense competition centered on growth, disputes between individuals or groups can become problematic. In this process, vulnerable populations are often excluded from decision-making and social inequality may widen.

Among numerous resources, land is a key resource that serves as a spatial basis for growth. While rational land development is beneficial for balanced growth, inefficient development destroys forests and ecosystems. Social disputes about land may also hamper growth. In this context, South Korea's experience in land management can provide valuable lessons. Having experienced the Korean War after liberation from the Japanese, Korea has achieved a compressed economic development over the past 70 years. It is the first country in the world that turned from a recipient state to a donor state. World Development Indicators (WDI) indicate that in 2019, South Korea was considered a high income nation that ranked twelfth among the largest economies in the world. During the course of the nation's growth, a wealth of experiences was accumulated in managing land use and conflicts and implementing land policies.

Land conflicts occur when the interests of individuals, groups, and/or the public authority collide over a limited land resource. This involves conflicting claims to land rights by two or more parties regarding the use or conversion of the land. Based on Wehrmann (2006), Deutsche Gesellschaft für Internationale Zusammenarbeit, also known as GIZ (2017), defined "land conflict" in the following manner:

> *"...at least two parties are involved and whose origins are differences in interests regarding a given piece of land – possibly aggravated by differences in the social position of the parties. Land conflicts imply different interests over one or several property rights to land: the right to use the land, to manage the land, to generate an income from the land, to exclude others from the land, to transfer it and the right to compensation for it. A land conflict, therefore, can be understood as a misuse, restriction or dispute over property rights to land."*

According to a survey conducted by the Korea International Cooperation Agency (KOICA) in 2015, approximately 60 percent of all civil lawsuits in a developing country like Vietnam were related to land issues. Furthermore, land compensation associated with domestic and foreign investment was one of the most frequent disputes, followed by taxation associated with the evaluation of land prices. Occasionally, land issues result in violent conflicts worldwide. The World Bank Group (WBG, 2019) reported that 65 percent of the conflicts occurring in fragile and violent countries have originated from land. Moreover, the risk of violence was substantial when the competing parties over land were organized groups.

The difficulties in resolving land conflicts have been reported in numerous parts of the world. For example, in developing countries, land disputes frequently arise during the course of infrastructure development. Typical issues involve conflicts about land ownership, boundary disputes, encroachment on public land, forced eviction of settlers with inadequate compensation, and real estate speculation. The consequences are negative effects on the economic, social, and ecological well-being of society. Disputes over lands are often due to fragile institutions, weak government capabilities, or the lack of public engagement. Resolving land conflicts and addressing land issues are important for inclusive development. These efforts are imperative for developing countries worldwide, who are suffering from the vulnerabilities of poverty, social inequality, and climate change. However, only a few studies have dealt with the experiences of countries like South Korea over the issue of land conflict resolution. This study fills the knowledge gap by evaluating Korea's experiences from a geospatial perspective and proposes land-based planning strategies.

In the book, we reviewed the literature dealing with South Korea's growth experience in relation to land management. We examined Korea's post-war restoration process and experiences in land development and conflict management over the last half century. Instability of land tenure, conflicts over securing land, problems in land use and management, conflicts between development and environmental conservation, issues of forced eviction, and a policy on the greenbelt were analyzed. Furthermore, the interests of different stakeholders in the conflict situation and civic participation were examined. The socially disadvantaged and vulnerable groups were identified in the analysis. The proposition is that the desirable state of inclusive growth in Korea was strongly supported by secured land tenure and careful management of land resources, which has been practiced over the last half-century. This study conducted in-depth interviews with six professionals in Korea's leading urban and regional development; environment, land, and spatial information management; and development cooperation. Finally, we outlined Korea's experience and expertise that can be learned by other countries with land conflicts.

Chapter 2

THE ROAD TO SUSTAINED GROWTH IN SOUTH KOREA

Instability in post-war Korea and rebuilding of the national economy

Korea has experienced remarkable progress in socioeconomic development over the past 70 years. In the 1950s and 60s, the key aims of the national policies were to support the restoration of damages caused by the Korean War and to lay the foundation for urban settlements and industrialization. After the post-war recovery, economic development focused on the government-led growth of light and heavy industries in the 1970s and 80s. Since the 1990s, as a countermeasure against the limitation of growth-oriented policies, the importance of sustainable growth involving the economy, environment, and society has become widely recognized. Such a change shifted the national development direction of Korea toward inclusive growth. This chapter reviews the key strategies, including geospatial approaches and land policies. In addition, the policy impacts are discussed.

Post-war reconstruction

After 35 years of Japanese occupation, Korea was liberated in 1945. But the period was followed by the outbreak of the Korean War between 1950 and 1953, and the social and economic damage was considerable. Due to the destruction of factories, power generation facilities, railways, houses, and agricultural lands, the nation's economic productivity had fallen dramatically. The sum

Figure 1. Destroyed buildings and war damages in Seoul (1950)
Source: Republic of Korea Armed Forces 2010

of the damage caused by the War was estimated to be $6.9 billion, which amounted to over five times the Gross domestic product (GDP) of the nation in 1953 (Chung, 2007). The impact led to a shortage in the supply of basic necessities for the livelihoods of the households. The wartime inflation was severe, such that consumer prices increased from 51.6 percent in 1949 to 230.2 percent in 1950, then to 232.6 percent in 1951 and to 112 percent in 1952 (Kim, 1995). During the economic turmoil, over 20 percent of the Korean population had to struggle for survival due to starvation and unemployment (Baek & Yun, 1991).

Beginning in the 1950s, a large number of migrants, refugees, and poor households moved to cities, thereby leading to an increase in the overall urban population. A rapid increase in urban density led to the spread of unlicensed houses and temporary tents in a number of vulnerable places. Unemployment and poverty were also significant. For example, jobless people in Seoul steadily increased after the war, soaring up to 23.2 percent in 1964 (The Seoul Institute; SI, 2020).

Stabilizing the society and rebuilding the national economy

CASE STUDY 1

Land policies in Korea and post-war recovery

The following were the major land management strategies during the post-war recovery period. First, the government clarified land ownership in rural areas through the Farmland Reform, which was enacted in 1950. By the time Korea was liberated, 77 percent of the total population was engaged in agriculture (Hankuk University of Foreign Studies; HUFS, 2013). However, this does not mean that engaging in farming was promising work. At the end of 1945, self-cultivating farmers accounted for only 14 percent of the nation's farmers (HUFS, 2013). Through reform, feudalistic tenant farming was ended based on the well-known principle of 'land-to-the-tiller.' This motivated the migration of rural populations to cities. The policy dismantled the old land tenure system by allowing tenant farmers to possess their own lands. Independent self-cultivating farmers with access to land could invest in agricultural productivity and educate their children, thereby contributing to the nation's modernization and industrial development.

Second, the ruined cities were efficiently restored through the Land Readjustment Project. The project, first introduced in 1928, was to develop the built-up areas by exchanging, subdividing, and combining the land without altering the fundamental ownership of the land. During the post-war restoration process, the project was conducted for rebuilding the urban infrastructure. Beginning in 1952, approximately 1,653 hectares of land were designated as a project district nationwide over a seven-year period, which contributed substantially to the restoration of the cities (Jung, 1994).

Third, the lack of financial resources was supported by the land tax. At that time, the Korean government needed to secure financial sources by increasing the land taxes in rural areas, where damage from the Korean War was relatively lower. The Decree on Land Tax, enacted in 1950 and revised over time, was implemented to increase Korea's tax revenue for the wartime and post-war budgets. Before the enactment of the law, the national tax revenue was less than 20 percent of the financial demand at the time, but by the Decree on Land Tax, the government's fiscal deficit was significantly reduced.

was the most pressing issue in Korea at the time. Like other developing countries, agriculture was the main industry in post-war Korea. Approximately 77 percent of the national population was dependent on agriculture for livelihoods. In this proportion, 86 percent were the so-called tenant farmers, who provided labor to landlords who owned a large farm (HUFS, 2013). The unfair socioeconomic structure of landlord-tenant relationship was an obstacle on the road to the mitigation of rural poverty. Moreover, at that time, the Korean industry had not yet fully developed, except for a few remaining factories that produced cement and fertilizers. The lack of an industrial infrastructure and skilled labor was problematic. According to Ryu (2017), in the absence of resources, Korea's economy relied heavily on foreign aid (over $3 billion) between 1945 and 1960. Overseas assistance helped to supply food and consumer goods to Korea, which at least temporarily stabilized the national economy. For example, between 1954 and 1959, the average rate of annual economic growth (based on Gross National Income) was 5.1 percent (Economic Statistics System; ECOS, 2020). The growth was associated with the recovery of agriculture during and after the Farmland Reform and manufacturing industries. By 1957, post-war recovery was at least moderately achieved (Seo, 2013).

Rapid economic growth and industrialization

After the initial period of recovery, Korea attempted to overcome widespread poverty by achieving economic development. State-led industrialization was a major policy vehicle. In the 1960s, light industries were developed based on the benefits of lowcost, hard-working labor. Consequently, the amount of exports of light-industry products – such as textiles, plywood, wigs, and shoes – increased dramatically. The manufacturing industry, which comprised a quarter of the total exports in the early 1960s, became a key driver of national economic growth, accounting for approximately 90 percent of the total exports in the early 1970s (Kim, 2014). Since then, the government also developed heavy industries, including

Figure 2. Guro industrial complex in Seoul
Source: The Seoul Research Data Service 2000

steel, petrochemical, automobile, shipbuilding, and machinery.

In the path of the Korean industrialization, it was necessary to provide infrastructure such as roads, housing, and ports. During the period, explosive urban growth was observed due to the migration of workers for employment and education opportunities. The rate of urbanization in South Korea, which was at 21.4 percent in 1950, increased to 56.7 percent in 1980 (Korean Statistical Information Service; KOSIS, United Nations; UN, Urbanization Rate, 2020). Highly dense urban environments generated a number of urban problems, such as the lack of social infrastructure, degraded sanitation, traffic congestion, and housing shortage. In the early 1960s, the national government took actions for improvement. Urban planning laws, such as the Building Act (1962), the Urban Planning Act (1962), and the Road Act (1961) were enacted. Based on the legal systems, a transportation infrastructure was built that included railroads and highways. Beginning with the construction of the Ulsan Industrial Complex in 1962, numerous state-led industrial complexes were planned and built. In addition, coastal areas with locational advantages were developed as a major industrial belt.

Spatially concentrated urbanization and industrialization caused unbalanced growth between the urban and rural areas. By the end of the 1970s, the central idea of national development was to concentrate investment in core cities – such as Seoul, Incheon, and Busan – as growth poles to efficiently utilize the limited land resources and financial capital. However, due to the issues of regional imbalance, in and around the 1980s, the growth of small and medium-sized cities near major cities was promoted. This led to the over-concentration of development projects in the metropolitan region of Seoul. Meanwhile, the Korean economy grew rapidly, at an average annual growth rate of 16.8 percent in the 1960s and 15.8 percent in the 1970s (National Geographic Information Institute; NGII, 2018).

Transition to inclusive growth

Since the 1990s, the goal of the economic growth in Korea shifted toward the pursuit of balanced growth and better quality of life. Political democratization was initiated with the introduction of a direct presidential election system and the dismissal of military authorities. The need for enhancing the competitiveness of Korea captured national attention, as there were limited growth-oriented policies that focused on the development of a few selected industries. Korea began to gain an international reputation, first with its economic growth marked as the Miracle of the Han River and touted as one of the so-called "Four Asian Tigers" and then with the hosting of the Asian Games and the 1988 Olympic Games. Furthermore, the nation opened its door to the world with the Uruguay Round Agreement and joined the Organization for Economic Cooperation and Development (OECD) in the 1990s. With a growing interest in enhancing the nation's competitiveness in the global market, high-tech industries were incubated. In addition, the overdensification of major cities like Seoul was relieved, at least partially, by implementing a reasonably effective new town program. The first-generation new towns such as Bundang and Ilsan were deployed near Seoul. In the early 1990s, numerous high-tech

Figure 3. The Han River in Seoul
Source: The Seoul Research Data Service 2015

businesses such as semiconductor, shipbuilding, and information technology became major industries in Korea. The following sections discuss the overall evaluation of Korea's growth in different sectors with a focus on the economic, social, and environmental sectors.

Economic growth

According to World Bank Group (WBG), as of 2018, South Korea is the 12th largest economy in the world based on GDP. By the end of 2020, South Korea's economy was ranked 10th in the world, surpassing the GDP of Russia and Australia. The average rate of GDP growth in Korea was at approximately 10 percent between 1960 and 1990. The rate decreased moderately to 7 percent in the 1990s and 4 percent after the 2000s. In 1960, the GDP was approximately $3,958 million; this increased by almost 400 times in 2019 to $1,646,739 million (WBG, 2020). The key driver for such exponential growth was the successful transition to industrialization. The development of the manufacturing industry has played a pivotal role in economic growth. The rate of employment (population over

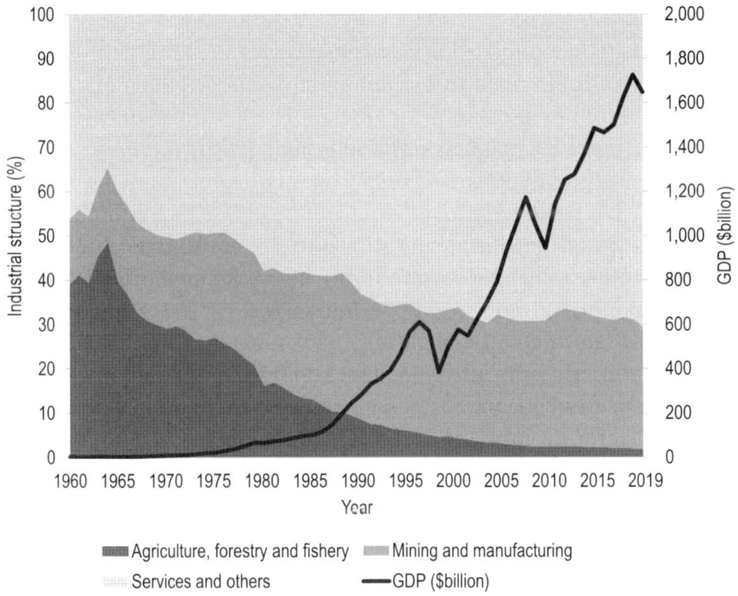

Figure 4. The change of industrial structure and GDP (1960-2019)

Source: Drawn based on ECOS 2020; WBG 2020

Notes: Korea's GDP (US$) is converted from domestic currencies using single year official exchange rates.

15 years) in Korea increased from 52.8 percent in 1965 to 60.7 percent in 2018 (KOSIS, Statistics Korea, 2021a), and the export growth rate was at an average of 37.4 percent in the 1970s, 14.6 percent in the 1980s, and 10.6 percent in the 1990s (Lee, 2009).

Furthermore, the effective development of key urban infrastructures such as roads, ports, railroads, and industrial complexes supported the nation's growth. The total length of the roads – which was only 28,145 kilometers in 1965 – extended to 110,714 kilometers in 2018 (KOSIS, Ministry of Land, Infrastructure and Transport; MOLIT, 2020). Simultaneously, with the first construction of the Ulsan Industrial Complex in 1962, approximately 1,212 national and local industrial complexes were built by 2019 (Korea Industrial Complex Corporation; KICC, 2020). In addition to the economic growth, dramatic urbanization has also occurred. The rate of urbanization was approximately 50 percent in the 1970s (KOSIS,

CASE STUDY 2

Expropriation of land for public and private uses

During the period of rapid economic growth, land had to be supplied for the provision of infrastructure, industrial complexes, and residential uses. Consequently, legal systems were established related to land expropriation. Based on such laws, a standard for claiming privately owned land was prepared for the benefit of the public. This greatly simplified the process of land expropriation.

The total area of expropriated land by the government between 1976 and 2018 amounted to 6,357 square kilometers, thereby accounting for 6.3 percent of the national land area (Korea Research Institute for Human Settlements; KRIHS, 2014b; MOLIT, 2019). Between 1980 and 2010, the annual average area of expropriated land was approximately 150 square kilometers, except for the year 2006 when large-scale land development projects were implemented (Lee, 2015).

UN, 2018, 2020). In 2019, over 90 percent of the total populations live in cities (KOSIS, Korea Land and Housing Corporation; LH, 2020). The Korean government implemented various urban policies, such as new town and redevelopment plans, to resolve the shortage of urban housing. Consequently, the total amount of housing increased by over three times from 4,734,000 in 1975 to 13,884,000 in 2010. Moreover, in the 2010s, the housing supply rate per capita exceeded 100 percent nationwide (NGII, 2018).

Since the 1980s, the Korean government has recognized the importance of research and development (R&D) for boosting the nation's economic growth. As a result of investment and incubation of human capital, Korea ranked 11th in terms of the Global Innovation Index (GII) in 2019, which measures the annual innovation ranking of 131 economies. This was the secondhighest place in Asia, after Singapore (Soumitra et al., 2019). This implies that Korea is one of the innovative countries that has the capacity for and success in innovation performance.

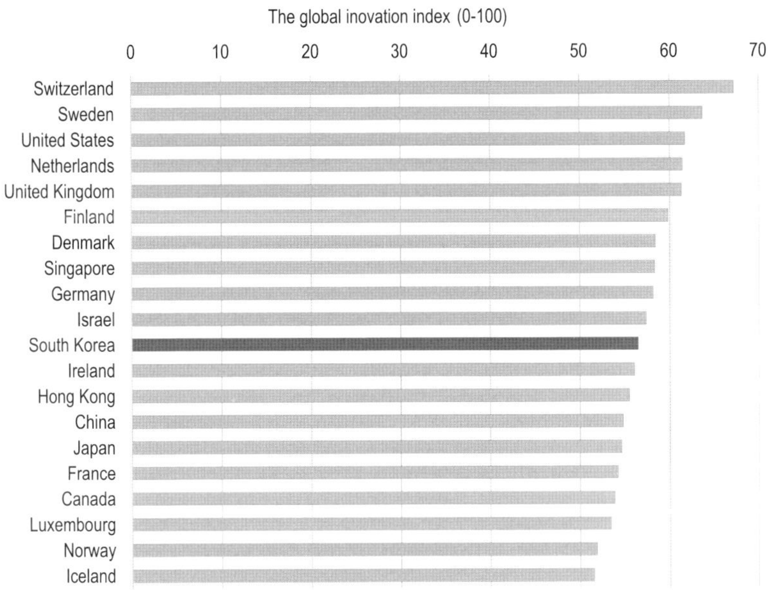

Figure 5. The global innovation index (2019)

Source: Drawn based on Soumitra et al. 2019

Notes: The Global Innovation Index (GII) is calculated by considering the following elements: 1) Innovation input sub-indices: Institutions, Human capital and research, Infrastructure, Market sophistication and Business sophistication, 2) Innovation output sub-indices: Knowledge and Creative outputs.

Based on innovative capacity, Korea has had notable success in numerous fields that can be attributed to the nation's growth. For example, the percentage of patents on the environmental technologies of Korea has already surpassed the average of the OECD countries in 2009 (OECD, 2016). The growing number of environmental patents had the capacity to promote Korea's green growth by developing new environmental industries with less damage to the environment. The introduction of an efficient public administration system also helped to innovate the country. The e-Government system prevented the unnecessary waste of fiscal resources in administrative works, thereby enabling efficient responses to civil complaints and prompt access to public resources.

Social development

Human capital – referring to the cumulative knowledge, skills, and experience of the people in a society – had a significant role in the growth of South Korea. According to the United Nations Development Programme (UNDP), the Human Development Index (measuring the life span, education level, and national income) of Korea has grown rapidly compared to that in the 1990s. The index, which remained at 0.73 in 1990, exceeded 0.9 in 2018 (UNDP, 2019). An increase in the education level was the most significant factor for Korea. With the introduction of compulsory elementary education between 1954 and 1959, educational opportunities expanded rapidly for all children in Korea. By 1959, the enrollment rate of all school-aged children rose to 96 percent from 64 percent in 1945 (HUFS, 2013). When examining the school entrance rate,

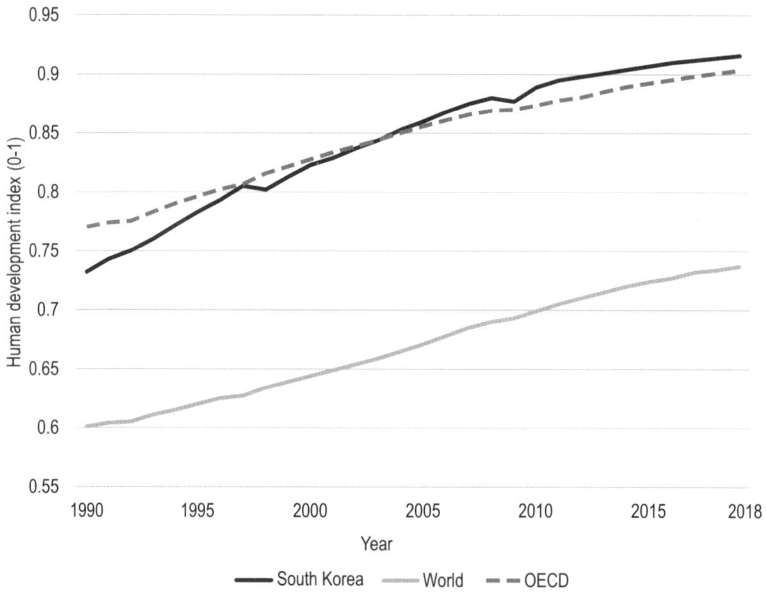

Figure 6. Human development index (1990-2018)

Source: Drawn based on UNDP 2019

Notes: The human development index is calculated as the geometric mean (equally weighted) of life expectancy, education, and GNI per capita between 0 and 1. The higher output value indicates a good country's overall achievement in social and economic dimensions.

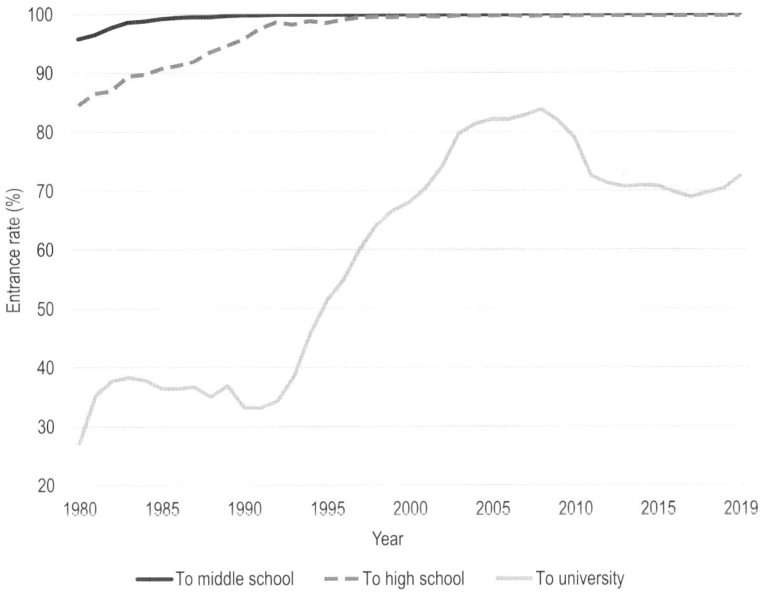

Figure 7. School entrance rate (1980-2019)

Source: Drawn based on Korean Educational Statistics Service (KESS) 2019

secondary and high school education reached almost 100 percent in the 1980s. All elementary and middle school children in Korea are mandated to stay in school. Beginning in 2021, all high school students in Korea are set to obtain free education. Moreover, the university enrollment rate had increased to almost 80 percent in 2008 (Heo, 2012). Although it decreased to almost 70 percent in 2020, Korea has the highest population with access to tertiary education among the OECD member countries (OECD, 2020a).

Social inequality remained rather problematic in Korea due to the legacy of growth-oriented development policies. According to the GINI coefficient measured by the OECD (2019), Korea (0.35) ranked tenth, following Mexico (0.46), USA (0.39), and UK (0.36), among the 37 OECD countries. In earlier years, the degree of inequality in Korea was far less problematic. The Gini coefficient fell from 0.33 to 0.28 between 1980 and 1997, which indicated a very low degree of income inequality. This decrease in the Gini coefficient implies that Korea became more unequal than before in

CASE STUDY 3

Development of human capital and the Farmland Reform

It is well known that fixing the unfair structure of land ownership affects the growth of a nation's human capital through educational attainment. In South Korea, the following factors have been discussed as the background of human capital development through the Farmland Reform (Park, 2015). First, by securing the economic foundation of independent farmers, the opportunity for educating the younger generation has increased. At the time, the reform enabled numerous farmers to use agricultural products, which previously had to be paid to the landlords as tenant fees, as payment to educate their children (Seo, 1987). Second, through the reform, the establishment of private school foundations was fostered. In the 1950s, an exception was included in the reform: a piece of land used for academic purposes. This exception contributed to an increase in the formation of private schools in rural areas. The total number of private schools prior to the reform was only 137 in 1947. This increased to 729 in 1957, thereby enabling the achievement of the goal of increasing the number of educational institutions.

terms of wealth distribution.

Inequality is found not only in terms of household income, but also in the distribution of property ownership. Individuals owning land property account for 33.4 percent of the total population, and 96.5 percent of the national private land is owned by a small proportion of the people with income in the top 10 percent bracket (Nam & Lee, 2020). Korea attempted to reduce this gap through various policy vehicles, including income tax and land tax. However, significant social inequality remains.

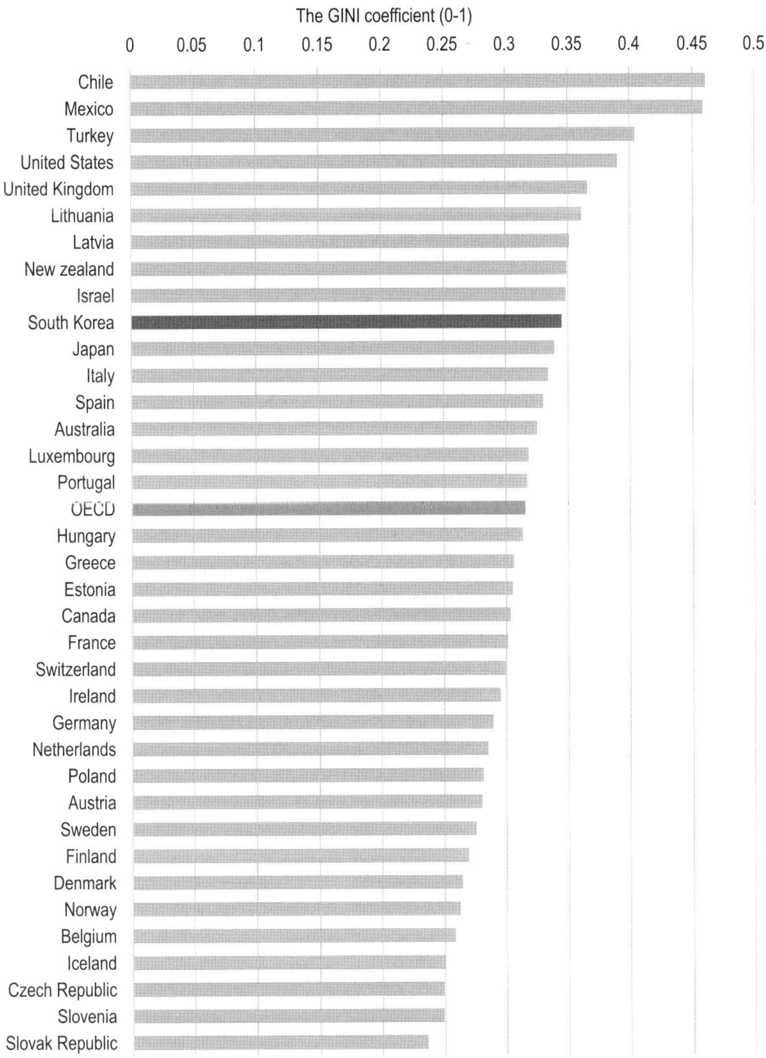

Figure 8. Income inequality in different countries (2019)

Source: Drawn based on OECD 2019

Notes: Since the GINI coefficient was measured in different years, the data for each country used the latest value measured between 2015 and 2019; The GINI coefficient is calculated based on the comparison of cumulative proportions of the population against cumulative proportions of income they receive. The index ranges between 0 and 1, and higher value indicates the case of perfect inequality.

Environmental preservation

Korea's rapid industrialization has significantly increased energy consumption. The primary energy consumption per person (equivalent to a ton of oil) increased by over five times from 1.18 in 1981 to 5.96 in 2018 (Korea Energy Economics Institute; KEEI, 2020). In addition, the amount of electricity (kilowatt-hour per person) increased by almost 10 times from 915 in 1981 to 10,195 in 2018. The increase in energy consumption has led to a dramatic increase in the emission of air pollutants, including greenhouse gases. According to WBG (2014), Korea's CO_2 emissions increased by approximately 2.5 times between 1990 and 2014. However, CO_2 emissions relative to the nation's GDP growth have decreased since the 1970s (OECD, 2020c). In addition, air pollutants such as sulfur dioxide, dust, and carbon monoxide continued to increase with the economic growth but began to decline since the 2000s (Korea University, 2014). Similarly, an increase in waste products has declined since the 1990s. The amount of waste per capita, which was approximately 714 kilograms in 1990, decreased to 368 kilograms in 2015 (OECD, 2020b).

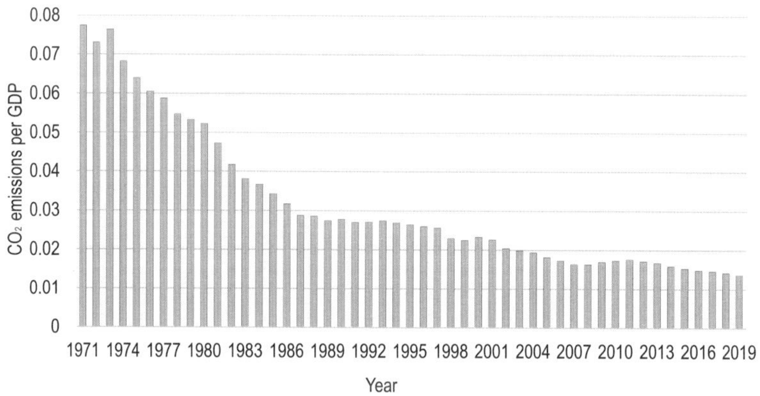

Figure 9. CO_2 emissions per GDP in Korea (1971-2019)

Source: Drawn based on OECD 2020c; OECD 2020d

Notes: The index is calculated based on CO_2 emissions (million tonnes) and GDP (US dollars/capita).

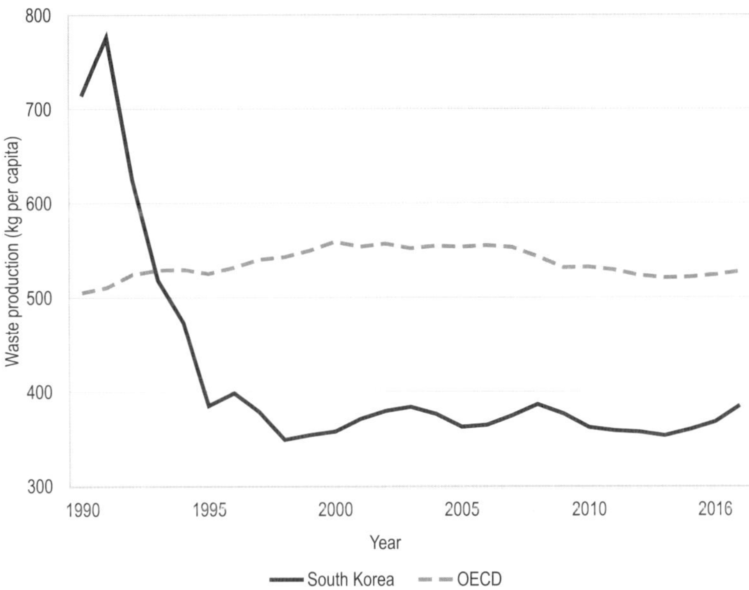

Figure 10. Waste production of Korea and the average of OECD (1990-2016)

Source: Drawn based on OECD 2020b

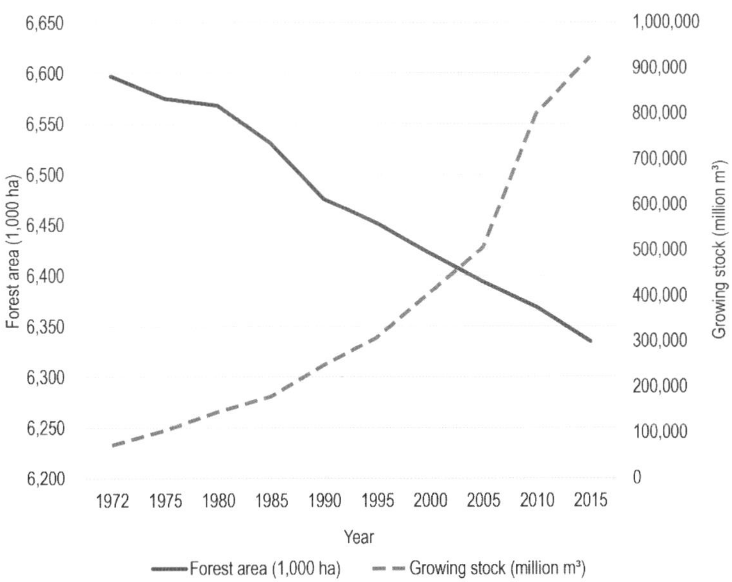

Figure 11. Forested area and growing stock in the forested land (1972-2015)

Source: Drawn based on Korea Forest Service (KFS) 2016

Notes: The growing stock means the volume of all living trees in a given area of forest or wooded land that have more than a certain diameter at breast height.

CASE STUDY 4

The green belt in Korea

The green belt was introduced in 1971 to limit uncontrolled urban sprawl by preventing the conversion of forested land to other uses. By 1977, a total of 5,397 square kilometers of land was designated, which accounted for 5.4 percent of the nation's land (MOLIT, 2011). In the area designated as the green belt, private activities are not allowed including building construction, work installation, and land transformation.

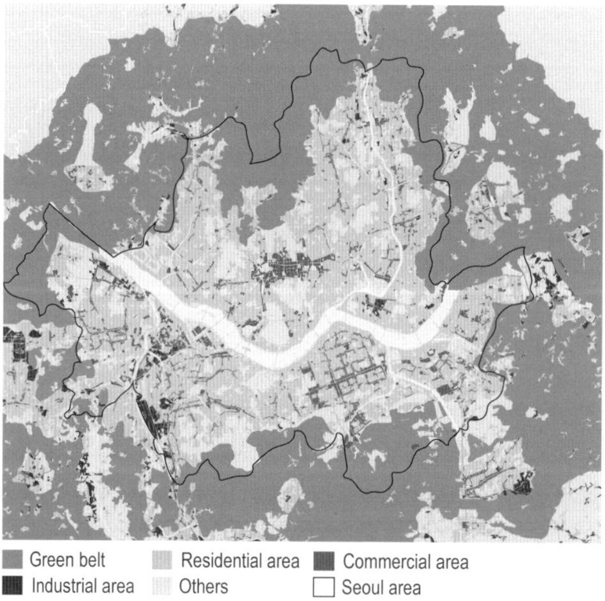

Figure 12. The green belt and a land use map of Seoul (2020)

Source: Drawn based on Korea National Spatial Data Infrastructure Portal (KNSIP) 2020

The green belt provided significant benefits, such as preventing the sprawl of urban areas, preserving ecosystems, preventing environmental disasters including flooding and landslides, improving the living environment of residents, and protecting the beauty of the green landscape. Despite these positive aspects, the side effects were also debated, including the issues of reasonable use/development of an area with little ecological benefits and the high administrative burden on local governments resulting from land disputes. The violation of land owners' property rights has been one of the critical issues in the areas designated as the green belt. Moreover, the strict regulation on development has worsened the quality of the residential environment in the green belt areas. Furthermore, despite the goal of the greenbelt to control urban sprawl, the development of suburban areas outside the green belt has expanded, thereby leading to an additional burden such as the development of infrastructure and transportation cost. In addition, even a formerly urbanized area with no ecological value was designated as the green belt. Nevertheless, the government has maintained the policy for over 20 years.

However, since 1990, the deregulation of the green belt has been carried out for multiple purposes. Due to several problems such as property rights, administrative burden due to management, and economic crisis, a change in the policy was necessary. In 2000, the Act on Special Measures for the Designation and Management of the Development Restriction Zones was enacted to release areas

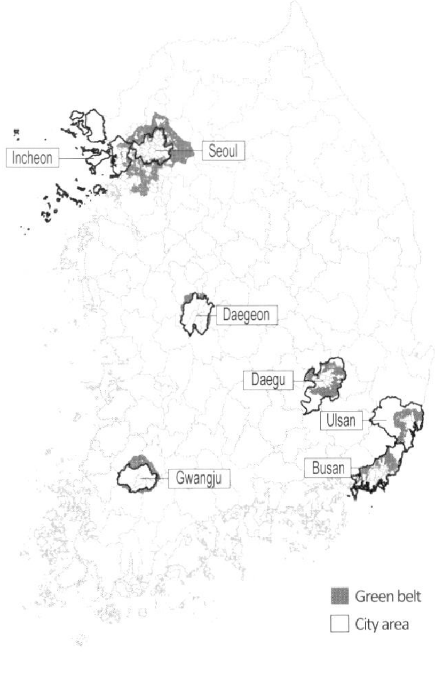

Figure 13. The green belt and metropolitan cities in Korea (2020)

Source: Drawn based on KNSIP 2020

with low conservation value for development. The release of the green belt was prioritized in cities with low potential risks of urban sprawl. Consequently, in 2011, the green belt area decreased to 2,895 square kilometers, accounting for 28 percent of the initial designated area (MOLIT, 2011). In metropolitan cities such as Seoul, only a partial relaxation of the regulation was done.

According to the Korea Forest Service (KFS), with 63.2 percent of the nation covered in forested areas, Korea is one of the countries that has the largest proportion of forested land among the OECD members. Forests in Korea were undermaintained in the early twentieth century. The deforestation rate reached 80 percent in the early 1960s, and the growing stock representing the total volume of trees was less than 10 cubic meters per hectare (National Institute of Forest Science; NIFS, 2014). In the absence of other energy sources, the consumption of forest for fuel accelerated, thereby resulting in extremely low land productivity in the forested areas. The Korean government sought to minimize the damage to forest resources through various activities, such as the introduction of Arbor Day, the establishment of the Forest Service, and the implementation of various forest conservation projects. Since the 1970s, large-scale tree planting projects were initiated, and slash-and-burn agriculture was banned. Consequently, the total number of trees in the forest increased to 146 cubic meters per hectare in 2015. Nevertheless, the forest area is continuing to decline due to the continued spread of built-up areas.

Chapter 3

POLICY INTERVENTION TOWARD SMART LAND USE AND MANAGEMENT

Rapid urbanization and urban problems

After the liberation, urban populations soared with an influx of war refugees, veterans, rural-to-urban migrants. The population of Seoul during the Korean War was approximately 0.6 million (Jun et al., 2007); between 1953 and 1960, the population increased to 2.45 million (Son, 2005). As the period was marked with social instability and weak land tenure, such rapid population increase posed serious problems (Kim, 2003). Meanwhile, damaged houses in Seoul in the aftermath of the war were affected approximately 53.4 percent of the total housing stock in 1953 (KOSIS, Statistics Korea, 2010). However, the supply of housing and social infrastructure could not accommodate the increasing population. As the demand for housing increased rapidly, housing prices skyrocketed. Urban migrants could not afford to buy or rent standard houses. They had no choice but to sit on unclaimed lands and built unauthorized wooden houses or temporary tents, thereby leading shantytowns in a hilly area or along the streams. Thus, the spread of illegal settlements on public land and property-related disputes were frequent.

According to housing statistics from 1953, the number of standard houses in Seoul was 133,232. The number of sub-standard houses was 123,472, including illegal houses (10,301), temporary accommodation facilities (397), and others like warehouses (1,542) (Jun et al., 2007). Refugees and farmers who moved to the city became the urban poor, encroaching on public lands and privatized

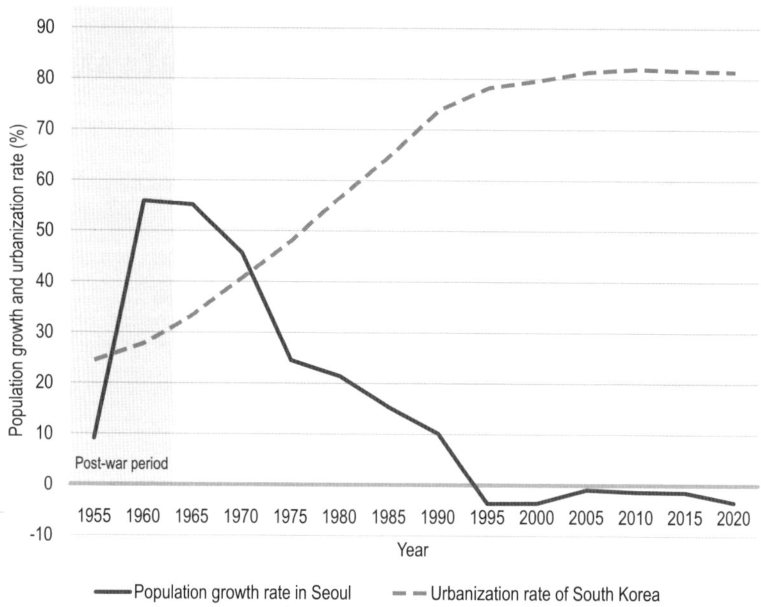

Figure 14. The rate of urbanization in Korea and the population growth rate in Seoul (1955-2020)

Source: Drawn based on KOSIS, Statistics Korea 2019; SI 2014; United Nations 2018
Note: Population growth rate was estimated in five-year increments.

territories. The unauthorized shantytown was not only an obstacle to rebuilding the urban area, but a place of fire hazards, floods, and poor sanitation. In the 1950s, the government implemented a coercive plan to demolish shantytowns. The settlers resisted unwanted relocation. If they had to, they moved to a nearby slum or another shantytown. Recognizing the limitations of the top-down demolition and eviction measure, the government began to implement a policy of creating a relocation town in 1959, beginning with the Miari Resettlement Town. The development of the Gwangju Resettlement Town is another example. Nevertheless, the ratio of the number of shanties in Seoul remained high, at 15.0 percent in 1961 and 37.8 percent in 1966 (Kim, 2003).

Further, due to the collapse of the industrial base, urban areas had insufficient jobs. There were approximately 1,297 industrial facilities in Seoul in 1946. In 1954, after the war, the number decreased by half (Kim, 2003). Statistics reveal that the national

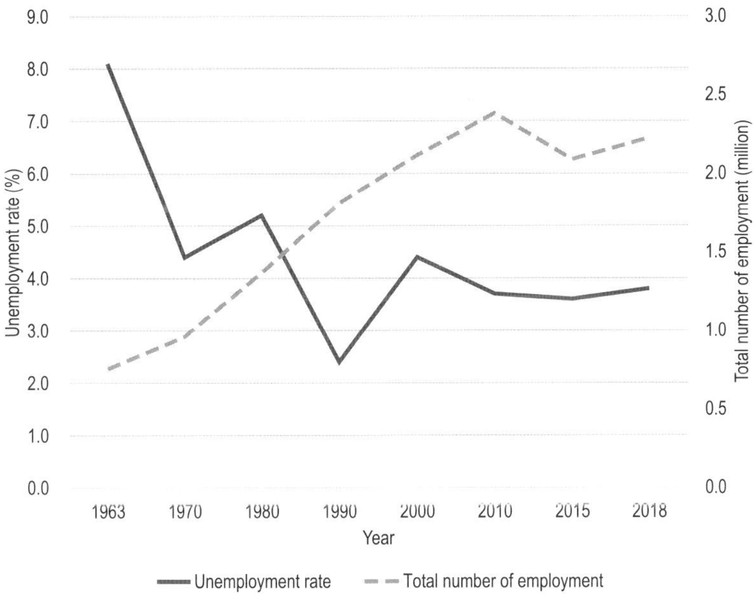

Figure 15. Unemployment rate and the total number of employments in Korea (1963-2018)

Source: Drawn based on KOSIS, Statistics Korea 2021a; KOSIS, Statistics Korea 2021b; The Economic Statistics Department of Bank of Korea 2005, 27

unemployment rate was the highest at 8.1 percent in 1963 and gradually decreased after the full-scale industrialization of the 1970s (The Economic Statistics Department of Bank of Korea, 2005). Besides, as rural labor left their land, the problem of food shortage became serious. Not only did this cause the people to suffer from poverty, but the nation's poor finance made it difficult to conduct post-war recovery. In addition, infrastructures were lost in the war. According to the statistics of the damage from the war, Seoul had lost 30.1 percent of the roads, 50.8 percent of the water supply facilities, and 66.1 percent of the erosion control facilities in 1953 (KOSIS, Statistics Korea, 1953a; 1953b; 1953c). People were frequently exposed to sanitation problems and disasters such as floods. In addition, the poor supply of infrastructure led to the construction of low quality houses.

It was required that the restoration of urban infrastructures be undertaken immediately. But people in the shantytown were not

Figure 16. Flooded area around Cheonggyecheon stream (1967)

Source: Seoul Metropolitan Archives 2018

prepared to move to other areas for infrastructural improvement. They remained in a backward condition, suffering from poor sanitation, a lack of clean water supply, and vulnerability to fires and floods. In the 1950s, the government's top priority was the restoration of the war-damaged district. Making roads and factories was also important. Clearing out the debris of the collapsed buildings was undertaken .

The land and forest survey project conducted under the Japanese period was the nation's first-of-a-kind modernized land survey. However, the survey documents were largely destroyed after the Korean War. The absence of basic land information, which was recorded in the form of cadastral maps, land registers, and forest registers made it difficult to understand the current use of the land. In addition, as large-scale urban development projects began to be implemented in the 1960s and 1970s, public records of land sale, acquisition, and merging of parcels were left undocumented. This, in turn, led to the failure of equitable land and property taxation, which unfairly profited a small number of real estate speculators.

The lack of land use and land management system was one of the main causes of the conflict. Due to the absence of land status data, information such as ownership, land boundary, area, and real estate transactions, etc. was not officially registered before the 1960s; thus, efficient land administration was not possible, thereby making it difficult to respond to various land disputes. In addition, due to the inadequate land market management system, speculation and land price hikes using real estate development were prevalent.

Documenting land and collecting information for public administration were required to manage land-related conflicts during the restoration period. Due to insufficient data and transaction registration system, the government had difficulty in grasping the exact size and scope of state-owned land and was unable to secure accurate taxes from private land. It was also difficult to manage private land to secure sites for public development. Meanwhile, in the event of a dispute on neighboring lands or compensation for the public development, the landowners and public administrators suffered from resolving the conflict.

As land development became active around the 1970s, the

polarization of wealth deepened, as private capitalists – who attempted to maximize surplus capital from the land transaction – preemptively bought a property for speculative purposes. In particular, real estate speculation caused land prices and sale prices to rise, making it difficult for ordinary citizens to own houses. One such case was found in Gangnam, where land development was initiated in 1966 with the announcement of the Yeongdong Development Plan. Speculators flocked to Maljuk Street, which was the starting point of the Gyeongbu Expressway. Although the government introduced the Act on Special Measures for the Prevention of Speculation in Real Estate in 1967, the opening of the Third Han River Bridge and the Gyeongbu Expressway caused the land price of the Maljuk area to soar from $0.36 per square meters in 1966 to $5.45 per square meters in 1968 (constant 2021 US$; Cho, 2004).

In addition, the land use system was divided into urban and non-urban areas before the 2000s, thereby causing problems of reckless expansion of the urban area. This encroached on mountainous and forested areas with high environmental preservation value. In 1993, the quasi-agricultural area (*junnonlimjiyeog* in Korean) was implemented in non-urban areas for the deregulation to contribute to housing and the establishment of factories. However, it was one of the most problematic zoning systems because the landuse plan was established only for urban areas. The increment of urban sprawl was accompanied by individual development. The next six years up until 1999, 26 percent of the total area of the quasi-agricultural area was for factory development and 14.2 percent for housing construction (Seo, 2000). Poor living conditions of the residents and environmental pollution around unplanned individual factories became a problem due to lack of infrastructure. In order to prevent this problem, the National Land Planning and Utilization Act was enacted in 2002 to integrate a landuse plan of urban and non-urban areas. In addition, in 2003, the growth management system was introduced to permit development within the range of infrastructure capacity.

Taken together, at the center of the land conflict was the problem of the system of registering and managing information related to lands, such as the status of ownership, the scope and scale of the lot, the transaction details, tax regulations, and regulations on the use of land.

Challenges of securing land for development

In the early 1960s, the Korean economy began to shift toward a manufacturing-oriented industrial structure. A large number of people moved to large cities with manufacturing jobs. To accommodate the people and growing industrial activities, public development was required to create industrial infrastructures, houses, and parks. In addition, public development projects such as new towns and industrial complexes were pursued. In the 1980s, rapid economic growth and urbanization continued, requiring large-scale development of housing and infrastructure. However, there were limits to buying land with different private ownerships.

To solve this problem, the public created a system to secure land quickly at a reasonable price. The public set the price of the land and consulted with the landowner on the purchase. In the process, there were frequent disagreements between the public and landowners over the difference in the value of the land. In turn, it was often not negotiated, and the public prepared the Land Expropriation Act to forcibly acquire land. Thus, landowners became dissatisfied with such unfair, one-sided deals.

An example of this dissatisfaction can be found in the case of Bongeunsa Temple. In 1970, the Seoul Metropolitan Government expropriated 31.5 hectares of land near Bongeunsa Temple area for the purpose of relocating the Ministry of Commerce and Industry. Despite opposition from Bongeunsa Temple, the ownership of the land was transferred to the government at $482,000 (constant 2021 US$). The government knew that the land price would soar afterward with the development of Gangnam area. In 2014, according to the Korea Electric Power Corporation, the land was resold to a private corporation called Hyundai Motor Company for $959 million (constant 2021 US$). Bongeunsa Temple claims that the government did not set the right price for acquiring the land (Online Bidding; Onbid, 2014).

In addition, there were various other parties with vested interests in the land – not only the landowners but also residents, tenants, and corporations. Thus, in addition to compensation for land with property rights, compensation for nearby residents and business owners was also required. Therefore, the Land Compensation Act, which was prepared by the public for compensation, considered various parties. It was planned not only to pay land costs to landowners but also to pay for relocation to tenants and compensate business owners for operating loss costs. However, the people, in general, did not understand the government-led unilateral land expropriation plans and low compensation costs. So, it was not easy to resolve the conflict due to differences of opinion regarding the method and amount of compensation.

Controversies over appropriate compensation have occurred repeatedly, until recently. The most prominent case was associated with the development of Yongsan area. In 2009, the redevelopment of Yongsan 4-district was decided upon. Consequently, the landowners, tenants, and business owners were forced out of the land. Thus, according to the legal regulations, the redevelopment association decided to pay compensation for three months of business suspension to business owners and to pay four months compensation for relocation to tenants. However, the tenants asked for more measures because the compensations were too small to support their living. In this disagreement, the conflict intensified and led to a massive fire.

Conflicts of land development and environmental preservation

During the country's urbanization, numerous cities expanded into non-urban lands such as natural areas and farmlands. As 70 percent of the country is made up of mountainous regions, damage to greenery was inevitable when an urbanized territory expanded outward. Encroachment on farmlands was extensive in rural areas. Priority for development was often given to obtaining development benefits, while overlooked the benefits of maintaining the farmland.

In particular, Korea lacked infrastructure facilities that could service scattered sites for housing and manufacturing. For this, power transmission towers were installed on the ridge, and hilly areas were flattened, thereby damaging the ecosystem and natural landscape. The large-scale housing development damaged nature by indiscriminately cutting hills or farmlands around the forest, causing disharmony of landscape, generation of wastewater, and emission of exhaust gas. Consequently, residents living near the damaged environment had to deal with the effects of such urbanization.

Forests were severely damaged through unauthorized deforestation and the illicit collection of forest products. In Korea, rapid development took place from the early 1970s to the late 1990s. In the process, asphalt and concrete replaced forests. Consequently, the forest area, which reached 6.61 million hectares in the 1970s, decreased to 6.42 million hectares in the 2000s. It has reduced by about 3 percent annually over the past 30 years (Ministry of Environment, 2014).

In Seoul, the damage was more serious. The percentage of the impervious areas – that is, the area covered with built-up land other than green space – increased 2.5 times from 18.4 percent to 47.2 percent (Kim, 2012). This development led to multiple types of environmental problems. The area damaged by landslides in the 1970s was 289 hectares, but in the 2000s, it increased to 713 hectares (KFS, 2013). Likewise, according to the annual disaster report, when comparing the 1970s and 2000s, the number of natural disasters – such as heavy rain, heat waves, and floods – increased due to the decrease in the green areas.

The proportion of paved land in Seoul is very high, which makes catching rainwater and surface runoff insufficient. The problem was exemplified in 2011, when a massive landslide occurred on Umyeon Mountain, located in the heart of Gangnam area, leading to 67 casualties (Seoul Metropolitan Government, 2017a). The local government, residents, experts, and civic groups were divided over the causes of the landslide. The Seoul Metropolitan Government and Seocho District Office attributed the landslides to torrential rains. The victims' families claimed that the landslide occurred due to the construction of the Seocho Tunnel and a park. As a result of an investigation by the Korean Geotechnical

Society, commissioned by the government, it turned out that the ground of Umyeon Mountain was weakened in the process of creating an apartment complex and a tunnel. It was also found that the artificially created drainage systems and embankment facilities were insufficient. The Supreme Court judged that the landslide on Umyeon Mountain was a natural disaster and a man-made one due to inadequate embankment facilities and a lack of guidance system. Consequently, the local government was sentenced to compensate the victims for the damage.

Smart land use and management experiences

Securing land tenure in shantytowns and establishing a relocation town

After the Korean war, the housing shortage was severe as the population in cities surged. The government promulgated a plan to provide housing relief. However, housing supply was far short, both quantitatively and qualitatively. The number of sub-standard houses and shantytowns increased steadily due to housing bubble and rent profiteering. National and public areas such as hillsides, riversides, and railroad tracks were occupied by early squatters. The displaced people who returned to Korea lived illegally on roads in the city center, such as Jongno 3-ga and Cheonggyecheon area, thereby creating a large-scale shantytown. This was a serious problem not only in Seoul but also in Busan (Jun et al., 2007). The spread of shantytowns was an obstacle to providing urban land services and other infrastructure. Poor sanitation, safety issues, and land tenure became problematic.

The problem of land ownership and *de facto* rights was a major conflict between the government and the urban poor. The government had to reconstruct the city with limited financial resources. On the other hand, poor urban residents attempted to solve the problem of housing shortage by building shantytowns in the city center or vending stuff on the roads to provide themselves self-rescue method for their tenure and right to live. Beginning in the 1950s, policy responses to the spread of shantytowns in Seoul and other cities were twofold: crackdown on illegal settlements and demolition of unlicensed houses. In 1954, the Seoul Metropolitan Government announced a plan to investigate illegal buildings, residing households, and unlicensed land occupation. However, implementing the policy to all the substandard houses in Korea was unachievable due to the lack of administrative capacity and qualified relocation settlements (Choi et al., 2015).

In the 1960s and early 1970s, a policy shift was made to demolish and resettle shantytowns. The intention was to provide at least minimum compensation measures to the urban poor in return for agreed relocation to a new location. The migrants had legal access to newly developed land so that they could begin a new life based on the basic means for livelihoods. After the 1970s, the Housing Improvement Redevelopment Project was enacted to implement housing renovation in shantytowns. In 1973, unauthorized shantytowns classified into redevelopment districts and demolition areas by the Act on Temporary Measures for the Promotion of Amelioration of Housing, laying the foundation of legalization for unauthorized buildings in redevelopment zones.

As securing public land for development in the city became difficult due to shantytowns, the government implemented a large-scale relocation policy to a new town in the suburbs of Seoul. In 1975, the introduction of the agency for international development loans allowed migrants to take out loans to pay for land purchases and housing improvements. The government was required to cover the initial costs of infrastructure development. Although the positions of the government and individuals were often at odds in the process of implementing demolition and relocation policies, the following outcomes were achieved.

- Legalization of the shantytowns: The readjustment of shantytowns in urban areas included compensation in the form of on-site legalization, subsidies for relocation, and the payment of the right to move into public housing built on state-owned land.

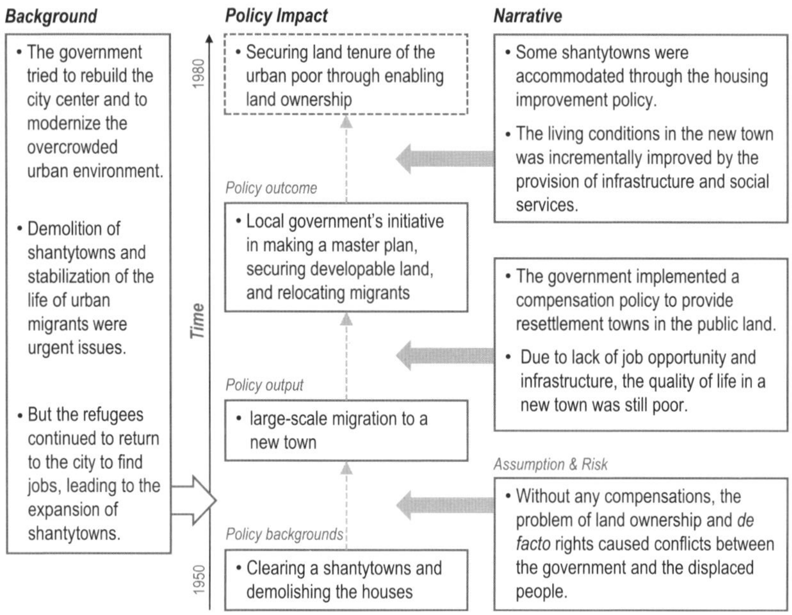

Figure 17. Contribution analysis of securing land tenure in shantytowns and establishing a relocation policy

- Restoring urban functions and securing developable land in urban areas: By demolishing shantytowns and expanding roads in downtown areas — such as Cheonggyecheon Stream, Yongsan-gu, Jung-gu, and Myeong-dong — the city was able to accommodate increased traffic volumes during industrialization (Jang, 1988). In addition, the government was able to supply housing complexes by securing development land in urban areas.

- Improving substandard housing and urban aesthetics: Despite the policy of legalizing shantytowns, the problem of poor housing continued, as people moved into the city in search of job opportunities. Along with the shantytown demolition project, the urban housing improvement project was implemented, thereby ameliorating the conditions of frequent flood and fire and improving urban aesthetics.

The basic idea of relocating slum residents to a new town with an opportunity for land ownership appeared to be a reasonable starting point for policy implementation. However, the results were not satisfactory due to the underestimation of the value of lands and properties that were formerly owned by displaced households as well as due to the very poor quality of living in the new settlements. Low-income households were not able to redeem the land that they were given as compensation, nor were they able to build a decent house on it at their own expense even in case of acquiring their land ownership. In addition, the "relocation first, then roads and services later" policy eliminated the lifeline of the settlers. Under these circumstances, they had no choice but to resell the land directly to speculators and returned to their original lifestyle of living in a slum. The widespread disappointment and indignation of relocated households led to a protest for protecting the resident's property rights. The struggle of Gwangju Resettlement Town (*Gwangju daedanji sageon*) in August 1971 is a case in point for the resettlement project. It gives a lesson that "slum clearance" must not end in the reproduction of fragility from one place to another. Therefore, it is important that the government create a habitable environment and secure land rights first and then implement relocation and resettlement plans.

CASE STUDY 5

Gwangju Resettlement Town

The Gwangju Resettlement Town project was implemented between 1969 and 1971. The government implemented a policy to relocate poor migrants living in the shantytowns of Seoul. This project was one of the largest housing complexes developed in the early 1970s, with 9.9 square kilometers in the former Gwangju Province of Gyeonggi-do (Lim, 2012). The Gwangju Resettlement Town is situated in the northern part of today's Seongnam.

Background

Many migrants, refugees, and poor households moved to cities like Seoul in the 1950s and 60s. The migration led to an increase in unlicensed houses and temporary tents (Kwon, 2012). Facing

A: Ruined housing in the aftermath of the Korean War (1950)
B: Demolition of unauthorized shantytown (Cheonggyecheon) (1965)
C: Gwangju Resettlement Town Residential village development (1970.09)
D: Gwangju Resettlement Town Residential village development (1970.12)

Figure 18. Background of the Gwangju Resettlement Town project
Source: A. National Archives of Korea 2021; B, C, D. Choi 2014a

substantial risks of poor sanitation, land use conflict, and safety issues, the local government announced a plan to demolish illegal settlements and relocate the *de facto* occupants to a resettlement town. Warning notices were given to the people in slums, followed by plans for demolition and compensation. Over 57,000 illegal houses were torn down, for example, along Cheonggyecheon and Yongsan Railway Station (Kim et al., 1996).

Although some compensation was made, displaced households from slums were frustrated. They lost their homes, and the amount of compensation was not sufficient, while the rent in the nearby neighborhood was relatively high. It drove numerous households back into slums in a different location. Facing numerous problems, bold action was taken by the government. One of the decisions was creating an entirely new town outside Seoul, targeting 200,000 (Son, 2003). The location was formerly called Gwangju Province, which is now part of the city of Seongnam.

Process

In May 1968, the Seoul Metropolitan Government implemented the project with the approval of the Ministry of Construction in under the Plan for the Construction of Gwangju Resettlement Town. To settle demolition migrants, the project involved an industrial complex for employment. In July 1968, the government purchased land, and in March 1969, the land development project was initiated. As land development commenced, relocated households were given the right to acquire a piece of land of 66 square meters with the term of a five-year redemption. The demolition began in May 1969. The project was promoted under the plan that electricity, water supply, and road facilities are provided. At the same time, each housing is built at the owner's own expense with partial subsidization from the government. However, due to hasty planning at that time, the relocation settlement was built in the form of a shantytown with no minimum facilities. There were no roads or waterworks at the time of relocation. Over time, the infrastructure investment plan was established in November 1969. As the poor residential environment improved, other people (non-migrants) began to enter the area, and resident certificates were resold. Due to the increase in the price of the resident registration card, numerous migrants had to sell their registration cards and return to Seoul. Therefore, the Seoul Metropolitan Government

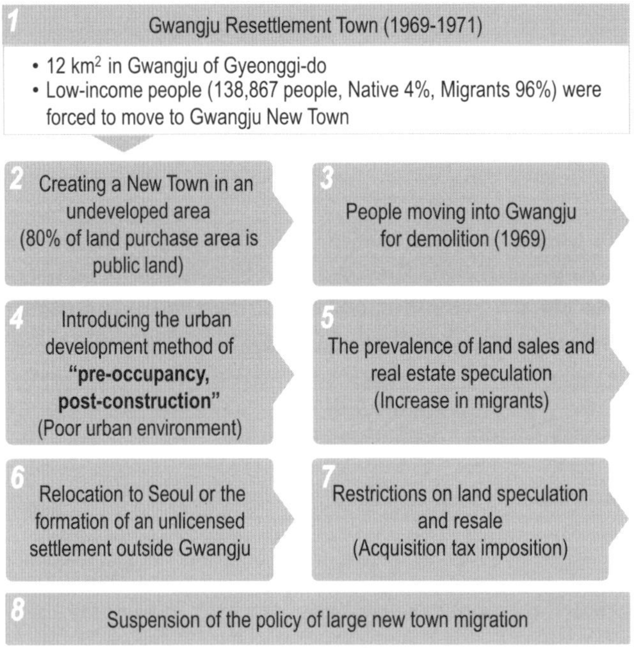

Figure 19. Process of the Gwangju Resettlement Town project

enforced a ban on the resale of resident registration certificates in July 1970. Due to a prohibition by the Seoul Metropolitan Government on the resale of occupancy certificates, the widespread disappointment led to a violent uprising in August 1971 (Kim & Choi, 2018). It began as a form of a petition for protecting the resident's property rights but soon evolved into a violent large-scale protest in the street, involving 30,000 to 60,000 people against the untrustworthy government (Lim, 2012).

The struggle was a turning point. The Seoul Metropolitan Government stepped back from the resettlement project, transferring the remaining land and properties to the provincial government, which served as a unified authority for assisting the inhabitants. Moreover, the unauthorized sale of land was prohibited, thereby leading to the stabilization of land prices. After the struggle, the Gwangju Resettlement Town project was transferred to Gyeonggi-do under the presidential order in July 1973. The administrative power concentrated in Gyeonggi-do spurred the building of infrastructure and the housing environment. This eventually led to the stabilization of housing in the area. In addition, through the establishment of the Seongnam Urban Basic Plan (1971-1990), it was possible to expand the construction of new cities. Since the 1970s, Gyeonggi-do secured its employment base by building industrial complexes in the resettlement project area. In 1971, Gwangju has deemed the first industrial complex, and in a mere six years, the industrial complex grew to employ over 30,000 people (Kim & Choi, 2018). In this sense, the Gwangju Resettlement Town became a self-sufficient new city, with a population of 300,000.

Problems and implications

Due to the principle of the "pre-settlement, post-development" method, problems of the poor urban environment such as the lack of transportation and infrastructure appeared in the early stages of resettlement. As migrants relocated to Seoul, the Gwangju Resettlement Town project failed as a large-scale settlement. In the case of developing countries, the "pre-settlement, post-development" method is not suitable. Hence, it is necessary to proceed with planned measures without rushing the project.

In the early stages of the Gwangju Resettlement Town project, the development project was delayed due to weak administrative power, and the residential environment was unstable. By unifying the business administration power to Gyeonggi-do, this project achieved residential stability and expanded the city (Kwon, 2012). The progress of a development project may slow down if several local/provincial governments (e.g., Seoul, Seongnam, and Gyeonggi-do) collaboratively manage the project. Therefore, it is necessary to promote the development project by concentrating administrative power and transferring the management system to one local government.

The Gwangju Resettlement Town project established an industrial complex from the early stages of development, settling and stabilizing some people in terms of job opportunities. By creating collective settlements and attracting the manufacturing industry simultaneously, the employment problems of migrants can be structurally solved. Therefore, it is necessary to create a job center suitable for the area when planning the development of a large new town.

CASE STUDY 6

The 104 Village redevelopment project

The 104 Village was formed in 1967, when residents in an unlicensed shantytown – who were pushed back by Seoul's urban development – moved in accordance with the state's compulsory migration policy. The demolition of shanty houses in the downtown areas of Yongsan-gu, Dongdaemun-gu, Seodaemun-gu, Cheonggyecheon, and Jungnangcheon forced 1,135 households to move to 104 Junggye-dong, Nowon-gu (Choi, 2014b). At that time, unlicensed housing in the city center was demolished under the Urban Planning Act to enhance urban aesthetics and restore urban functions. The residents of the demolished buildings were each given 25 square meters of state-owned land outside the city as settlements, but the residents themselves had to solve the lack of provision of other facilities because roads, water supply, and sewerage were not planned. The 104 village houses were built by residents themselves using materials in the surrounding areas. They had to also draw water and slate wooden skeletons. Although these houses have been aging for decades, various restrictions such as the designation of military facilities protection zones (1969) and the decision of the green belt (1971) have made it difficult to renovate

Figure 20. 104 Village
Source: Seoul Museum of History 2012, 244

or expand these housings, since there was expected to be numerous disputes over development benefits (Seoul Museum of History, 2012).

The need for redevelopment of 104 villages began to be discussed in the late 1980s, but the process was not smooth. Housing redevelopment projects were concentrated on generating large development profits, and 104 villages were excluded from the redevelopment projects in the 1980s and 90s, even though the surrounding areas were included. This is because there were a large number of unlicensed houses on national land and it was expected that there would be numerous disputes over development profits, as this land was designated as a development restriction zone. In 2010, the government decided to implement the public manager system and announced a system for the government to actively intervene in redevelopment projects.

In line with the government's policy, the Seoul Metropolitan Government announced a redevelopment plan for 104 villages in 2012 (Seoul Metropolitan Government Announcement No. 2012-159). After complete demolition, a few areas (42,773 square meters of the 188,900 square meters) were designated as Residential Preservation Zones (RPZ) to create housing centered on lowrise residential areas rather than a uniform apartment construction method that would be implemented under the existing redevelopment projects. The migration policy for tenants in 104 villages is offered on better terms than those in other

Figure 21. 104 Village redevelopment plan (2012)
Source: Seoul Metropolitan Government 2012

redevelopment areas. The details of the relocation policy include the payment of relocation costs, the guarantee of rental apartments to be used as temporary residences, and the guarantee of relocation to multi-family homes in RPZ after redevelopment. However, it remains unclear until now whether this "beautiful" plan will be implemented. This is because the confrontation between the interests of redevelopment and the public is still ongoing. In 2019, the redevelopment plan for a 20-story high-rise apartment was reprepared, but there are still numerous steps to be taken. Residents feel tired of the redevelopment discussion, which has continued for over 30 years.

The following are the stakeholders who have opinions on the redevelopment of 104 villages: the Residents' Representative Committee (RRC), which can select a project implementer and is legally granted the right to represent a house owner; the Seoul Metropolitan Government and Nowon District Office, which have the authority to apply for the project and approve the redevelopment after deliberation; the Emergency Planning Committee (EPC) that can push ahead with rapid development; and the Tenant Representative Committee (TRC). Each of these entities has a different strategic relationship depending on their business interests and political purposes, adjusting the direction and speed of the redevelopment of 104 villages.

The RRC insists on securing profitability from the redevelopment. They claim that the ratio of households to building rental houses in redevelopment areas proposed by the Seoul Metropolitan Government is unrealistic in terms of profitability and this must be reduced to 17 percent from 50 percent. The Seoul Metropolitan Government and Nowon District Office also want to push ahead with the redevelopment as soon as possible, but the redevelopment has been delayed as the Seoul Metropolitan Government has views that oppose that of the RRC over the housing conservation ratio. The claim by the Seoul Metropolitan Government and Nowon District Office is that since the development restrictions of 104 villages have been lifted, they must make as much "public contribution" by building more apartments or increasing the floor area ratio. The 104 villages have been subject to comparatively more lenient measures and asking for the easing of more restrictions would be inconsistent with current policies.

Although the EPC and TRC have different positions and profits to be gained, they are united in the launch of rapid redevelopment.

The EPC appears to have a large number of outsiders, and the TRC appears to have a large number of actual residents. However, strictly speaking, the TRC's tenants are also divided into "strategic tenants" and "pure tenants." A strategic tenant lives in 104 villages to receive the so-called "certificate" – that is, the right to move into a rental house or to receive support for relocation expenses, while a pure tenant lives in 104 villages and meets the requirement of redevelopment based on the tenant's residence. From the TRC's point of view, RPZ is essential for residential rights. However, from the EPC's perspective, where many bought land or houses on loans to live in apartments, the longer the time gap, the greater the interest and burden on loans; hence, it was preferred to push ahead with the redevelopment.

In addition, 104 villages have been portrayed in the media as valuable places of preservation representing "villages" and "communities." This has led to the publication of storytelling books for tourism in 104 villages, the appearance of photo exhibitions, alley tours, and murals since 2012. However, the irony is that while the appearance of RPZ through the policies and programs of the Seoul Metropolitan Government and Nowon District Office is being preserved with respect to human life and history, the houses in 104 villages are now tied to redevelopment and cannot be repaired, and tenants are living under dangerous conditions of deteriorating empty houses.

As of today, there is little discussion about people who will live in or be forced out of the residential areas while the stakeholders unite and fight for business interests. Property rights are often prioritized over housing rights in the redevelopment area. After over two decades of being swayed by external influences of redevelopment, residents are losing their right to participate in the area where they have vested interest for a long time. This is because the owners who do not reside in the redevelopment zones are classified as residents, but tenants who lived in the area for decades are not considered official residents.

These tenants are the actual residents who had lived in 104 villages and were required to return after the redevelopment. Above all, they are the current residents of 104 villages. However, their identity and narratives have been obscured, only to be selectively revealed depending on the overall redevelopment project direction and strategy.

The 104 Village case is summarized based on Jang (2014).

Redistributing rural lands and fixing the oligopolistic concentration of urban lands

After the Korean War, the Farmland Reform was not only a policy vehicle in restructuring the unequal land ownership in rural areas but also an important political task for the establishment of the country's democratic system. Although there was resistance from the landlord class, it was difficult for the landlord class to raise their political voices during the U.S. military regime after liberation due to their pro-Japanese activities during the Japanese colonial period. Industrialization was conducted stably after the reform, marking the era of development growth. In the 1960s and the 70s, land speculation was prevalent to gain land development profits. In the 1980s, development projects and speculation intensified in line with the hosting of the 1988 Olympic Games. Moreover, according to the survey on ownership of private land nationwide at that time, the top 5 percent of the population occupied 65.2 percent of the land (Choi, 2018). Make not only Land ownership for the capital accumulation be difficult to secure land necessary for industrial development, but also acted as a barrier to housing supply, thus hindering the supply of land necessary for the land market.

The followings were the main objectives of reorganizing the land ownership structure in Korea. First, addressing the unequal distribution of wealth and improving the unreasonable competitive structure of the land market was important. Second, the government sought to realize the principle of practical equality by curbing the accumulation and hereditary succession of assets. By doing so, the landuse efficiency increased by supplying the land held by individuals or private corporations to the land market.

With the implementation of the Farmland Reform Act in 1950, the ownership structure was transformed by restricting the qualification for owning farmland. The government intervened in the distribution as a mediator in two ways. One was with regard to decisions on the farms that needed to be redistributed and the determination of independent farmers having the right to acquire the land. The Farmland Reform Act limited landowners' ownership of farmland to less than 3 hectares and introduced a certification system for farmland acquisition so that land could be distributed to farmers who were able to actually cultivate the land for food production. The other was about how the land value is assessed and payment was made between two parties. In addition, the Farmland Committee – consisting of one public official, three landowners, and three tenant farmers – was established to enable the participation of tenant farmers in the democratic process of farmland reformation.

Meanwhile, in 1950, the Inheritance Tax Act and Gift Tax Act were introduced in urban areas to prevent the accumulation of development profits through inheritance without any costs or taxation. In order to prevent companies that accumulated capital due to continuous economic growth from owning land for speculative purposes with surplus capital, the government introduced a system to impose 7.5 times acquisition tax and 25 times property tax on non-business land under the Presidential Decree in 1974 (KRIHS, 2010). Based on this, the Land Excess Profits Tax Act was implemented in the 1980s with the introduction of the public concept of land ownership. The Ceilings on the Ownership of Housing Sites Act was introduced to prevent monopoly in the case of housing supply land. The Restitution of Development Gains Act was also enacted to prevent excessive privatization of development gains. In addition, various tax policies were introduced, such as property holding taxes levied on owning buildings and land above a certain standard, transaction taxes, and gift taxes levied on the occurrence of ownership transfer following the acquisition or transfer of the real estate. The following achievements were realized through restrictions on farmland ownership, excessive land ownership of urban land, and the taxation system.

- Tenant farmers transformed into self-cultivating farmers with assets on land: In 1947, the ratio of self-cultivating farmers was 17 percent, but in 1951, it increased to 81 percent after the Farmland Reform (HUFS, 2013). Self-cultivating farmers became dominant economic players in rural areas. Thus, poverty in rural areas decreased and the quality of life of farmers improved.

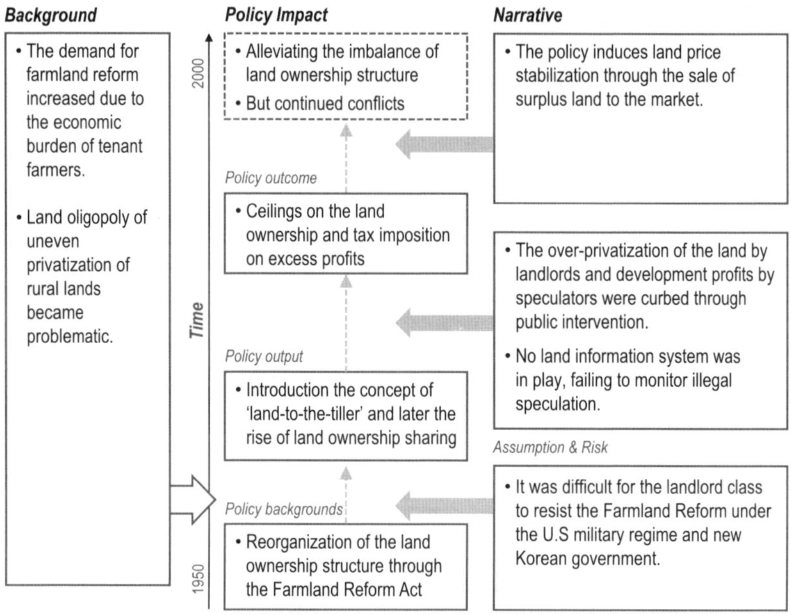

Figure 22. Contribution analysis of fixing the oligopolistic structure of land ownership

- Controlling land prices of residential real estate and normalizing housing supply: Limitation on the ownership of housing sites in housing development project districts stabilized the land price and normalized housing supply.
- Controlling capital accumulation through the oligopoly of land by enterprises: By regulating the acquisition of development profits and capital accumulation based on excessive non-business land ownership by chaebol companies, sound reinvestment of industrial capital was induced and there was fair competition among companies.

By dissolving the landlord class, the Farmland Reform resolved the problem of inequality among tenant farmers and laid the foundation for the growth of capitalistic land management. While the Farmland Reform in Korea is considered a success story, the increase in agricultural productivity was below expectation. At

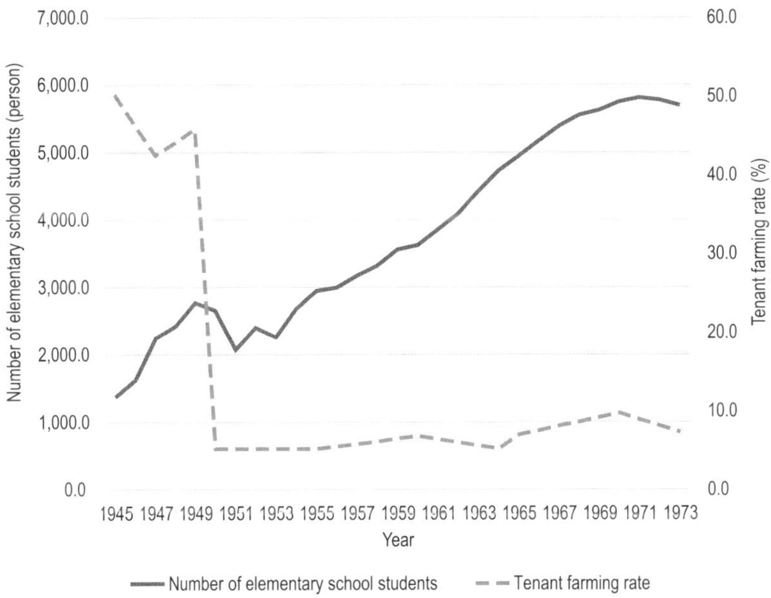

Figure 23. Tenant farming rate and the number of elementary schools (1945-1973)
Source: Drawn based on HUFS 2013, 110, 123

that time, self-cultivating farmers were incapable of cultivating a piece of land larger than 2 hectares because of limited agricultural technology. However, due to the resistance from landowners and wealthy farmers, the limit of ownership was adjusted from 2 to 3 hectares. The productivity and land ownership of self-cultivating farmers were secured at lowest level.

The other side of the reform was the risks faced by the former landlords. The landlords were compensated by land bills, but the value of the bill declined substantially due to war-time inflation. The initial attempt to turn the former landlords into entrepreneurs in emerging industries required time and coordinated effort. As the Korean society was not well prepared, however, the transition was not successful. Yet some landlords attempted to retain their influence on the rural economy. As a way of avoiding the loss of land ownership, some landlords established educational foundations in rural areas and endowed the land to those. This led to an increase in the number of schools and universities, making them an integral part of the public and private educational systems in Korea.

On the other hand, the housing ownership cap and development levy system were introduced to prevent the sale of small businesses in urban areas after industrialization achieved the effect of curbing speculation and over-holding of housing sites but did not last long. Due to the financial crisis of the International Monetary Fund, the demand for revitalizing the land market increased further and there was strong criticism that restrictions on housing ownership violate market economic principles. Restrictions on ownership of enterprises of non-business land had also phased out in the process of overcoming the Asian financial crisis and abolished in 2001.

Securing land for development: The Land Readjustment Project

After the war, there was not sufficient land and financial resources to reorganize the urban environment. To complement this, Housing Site Development was implemented based on the Land Readjustment Project by referring to the Chosun Urban Planning Ordinance, the first modern urban planning law.

The Land Readjustment Project consists of three steps: planning, development, and replotting. First, a specific area of an unmaintained city area is divided, and the land is provided free-of-charge from all landowners in the area to the public. Then, the public plans public facilities such as roads and parks at the appropriate scale at the required location with this funding. In this process, the land for each lot is designed, and the area of land secured by the authorities in recompense of development outlay is designated. After land development is implemented under this plan, landowners can take the replotting land and balance accounts in terms of the cost for the change in land value. When this process is over, the project is deemed complete. The Land Readjustment Project increased land use value more than before by changing the compartment or characteristics of land according to the readjustment of public facilities. It was an efficient urban development project that could improve land and increase its value without land and development costs.

Due to the Five-Year Economic Development Plan initiated in the 1960s, the population and industry were concentrated in the city as high economic growth continued. Accordingly, as urbanization took place rapidly, the demand for residential and factory sites quickly increased. To create a large number of housing sites, the Land Readjustment Project had to be actively employed. However, initially included the Land Readjustment Project in the Urban Planning Act and the Act on Farmland Improvement, respectively, so there has been confusion as both laws are used interchangeably. Therefore, there was a limit to the rapid supply of land to various development projects and the Land Readjustment Project under the existing Acts. Consequently, the Land Readjustment Project Act was enacted as an independent Act in 1966.

Until the early 1970s, most of the Housing Construction Projects were centered on constructing detached houses, and the Land Readjustment Project was mainly implemented as part of this process. However, in the aftermath of the industrialization policy promoted in the 1970s, there was a rapid increase in the urban population and the aggravated housing shortage in Seoul and other metropolitan areas.

Moreover, as apartment complexes built for land use efficiency gained explosive popularity, apartment-oriented housing supply policies were further strengthened. Accordingly, the Land Readjustment Project Act, which was centered on detached houses, was supplemented to enable the development of apartment complexes even in detached housing areas. In 1975, the Land Readjustment Project Act was revised to designate a large proportion of an area of land secured by the authorities as a recompense of development outlay to secure apartment land.

The Land Readjustment Project was a typical means for developing high-quality housing sites and planning urban areas until the early 1980s before the Housing Site Development Project began in earnest. It was a project based on the adjustment of land relations and was almost the only means of housing development before implemented the Housing Site Development Project. The main features of the Land Readjustment Project, which actively

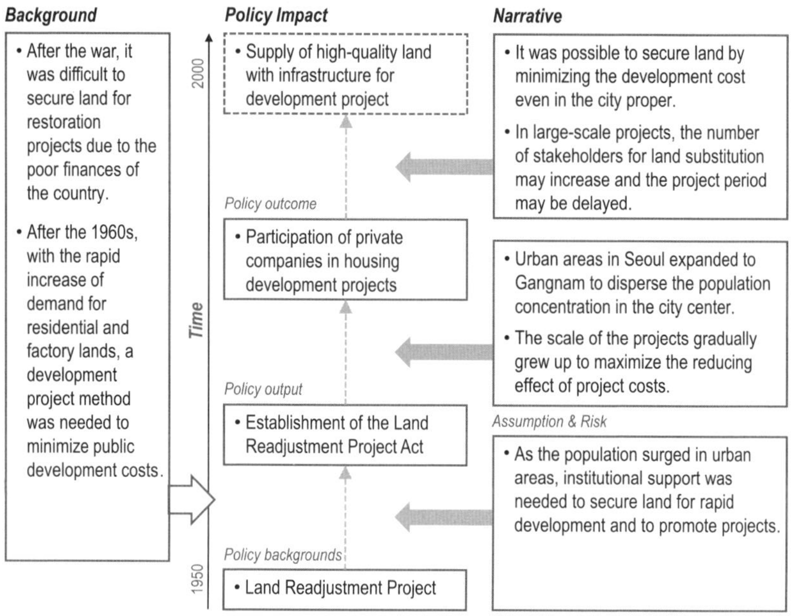

Figure 24. Contribution analysis of securing land for development

used until the early 1980s, are enumerated below:

- It was suitable as a city development method in the early stages of development when finance and land were scarce. In particular, it was a land development system that accommodated the population rushing to urbanization after the 1960s.
- It could be implemented in both new and old cities, and could maintain public facilities and urban planning facilities simultaneously.
- According to data from the National Archives of Korea, approximately 436 square kilometers of land in 397 districts nationwide were developed as the Land Readjustment Project by 1984. In the Seoul Metropolitan Government, a total of 93 square kilometers of residential land and 41 square kilometers of public land were developed as part of the Land Readjustment Project. It accounted for a large proportion

of Seoul's existing development area of approximately 35 percent.

- As such, the Land Readjustment Project has been a suitable development method for Korea since the 1960s, when land and development costs were scarce. In addition, this method prevented disorderly urban expansion and secured public facilities to enable systematic urban development.

Unfortunately, the Land Readjustment Project had limitations in terms of development period and area. In the aftermath of the industrialization policy promoted in the 1970s, the urban population rapidly increased, and the housing shortage in Seoul and other metropolitan areas was intensifying. Consequently, there was a limit to the Land Readjustment Project, which effectively constructed detached houses. Thus, in 1980, the Housing Site Development Promotion Act was enacted to provide high-quality, large-scale residential land. Eventually, the Land Readjustment Project was relatively reduced in volume, and its role became ambiguous as other land development projects emerged. Consequently, incorporated similar urban planning and development projects into the Urban Development Act in 2000, and the Land Readjustment Project Act was abolished. However, the main contents of the planning, development, and replotting for the implementation of the Land Readjustment Project have been passed on to the Urban Development Act and are still used today.

CASE STUDY 7

Housing provision through the Land Readjustment Project

The Land Readjustment Project was implemented to prevent the disorderly spread of urban areas and secure public land in advance to develop a new urban area without transferring the former land ownership to land speculators. The project is a type of replotting method for exchanging or dividing land without a change in land rights set before the project's implementation (Kim, 2015). The method provides large-scale privately-owned housing, while minimizing the input of public investment. It can also reduce land conflicts because the original landowners regain the land title with new infrastructure at the end of the project. Public spaces can be secured in advance and have the advantage that the value of land use can be increased through the reorganization of the area. Therefore, this method is suitable as an urban development method when public finance is insufficient. It is effective not only in the regions that are not urbanized but also in established cities.

Korea's Land Readjustment Project began in 1934 under the Joseon City Planning Ordinance. With the enactment of the Land Readjustment Project Act in 1966, Korea's Land Readjustment Projects in the 1960s and 70s were somewhat active. It usually gave priority to landowners and unions (Kim, 2015). If the Land Readjustment Project's implementer does not prioritize landowner and the union, the implementer – the state, local government, Korea Housing Corporation, Korea Land Development Corporation, etc. – could become the land developer. Korea's Land Readjustment Project led to a total area of 480 districts in 1989, covering 461 square kilometers (140 square kilometers in Seoul) (Seoul Metropolitan Government, 1989). The Land Readjustment Project was actively conducted in metropolitan areas with high population concentration.

The role of Korea Housing Corporation

Korea Housing Corporation is an institution that provides housing and manages it through corporate methods by investing a certain amount of capital. The purpose of the corporation is to build and supply sustainable housing. The Korea Housing Corporation, established in 1962, built the first apartments in Korea. In 1966, the Land Readjustment Project Act was enacted, and the Korea Housing Corporation initiated the Land Readjustment Project in 1967 (KRIHS, 2011). It implemented three land compartmentalization districts in Seoul: Hwagok, Gaebong I, and Gaebong II (Seoul Metropolitan Government, 1989). The Korea Housing Corporation supplied public housing, public rental housing, permanent rental housing, and national rental housing and implemented housing construction plans, housing site development projects, and urban readjustment projects by region.

The Land Readjustment Project in Hwagok district

The Land Readjustment Project of Hwagok district is located in Hwagok-dong, Gangseo-gu, Seoul, Korea. The project area is 1,025,142 square meters and it was implemented from 1967 to 1970 by the Korea Housing Corporation (Seoul Metropolitan Government, 2017b). The current urban structure of the Hwagok district is the same as it was implemented in the Land Readjustment Project. Public facilities such as schools, hospitals, and dormitories are still well maintained in the Hwagok district. Hwagok district could be developed without significant conflicts as a place for multi-family housing due to the well-established urban structure introduced from the beginning of the project. Due to the satisfactory infrastructure, small-scale development of parcels is possible.

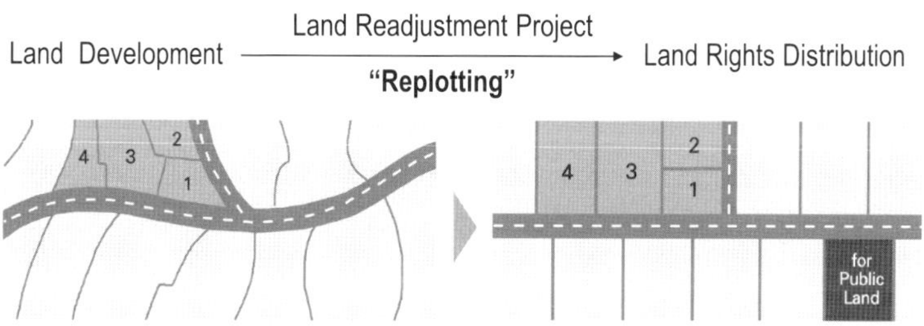

Figure 25. Replotting method of the Land Readjustment Project

Source: Drawn based on Seoul Metropolitan Urban Planning Bureau 2016

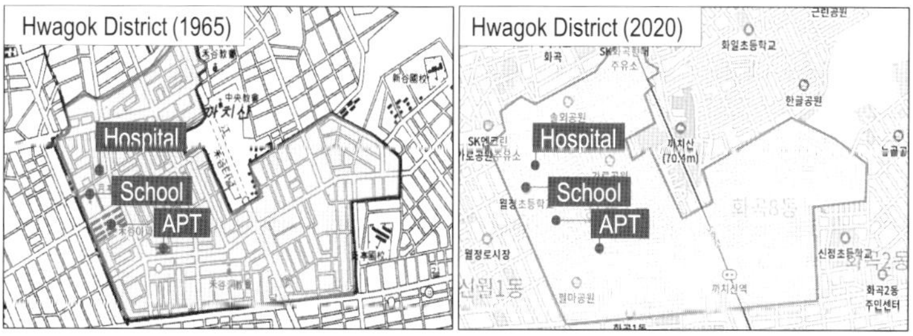

Figure 26. Changes in the urban organization of Hwagok district Land Readjustment Project (Comparison between 1965 and 2020)

Source: Drawn based on Seoul Metropolitan Government 2020

Managing land markets and digitizing land-related information

The first cadastral survey was conducted during the Japanese colonial period. After the Korean War, a large amount of cadastral information was lost. Some were reconstructed for military purposes during the US military regime, however, the cadastral information was unclear. In the 1960s, the Korean economy began to shift toward industrialization, leading to the rise of the demand for land information. The unclear land boundaries, inaccurate land valuation, and the absence of a land transaction registration system became problematic.

When the boundary information of the parcel is not clear, compensation problems arose between the landowner and the developer, or ownership conflicts arose between the landowners. In addition, due to the lack of a land management system, it was difficult to check the records of land transactions and trace the real estate speculation. This led to the land price increase in the development area. Since the announcement of the Ulsan Industrial Complex Development Plan in 1962 and the construction of the Gyeongbu Expressway in 1967, the rate of land price increase in 1969 reached 80.7 percent nationwide and 84.1 percent in Seoul (KRIHS, 2010). This increase in land prices caused social problems of privatization and polarization of development profits. In the 1970s and 1980s, various policy measures, including the land transaction permit system and reporting system, were introduced to deter speculation in real estate. However, illegal transactions, speculation, and tax evasion did not subside. These problems led to the officially assessed land price system, an index to calculate excess profits and development charges for land development, has been established. The system unifies land prices as one standard. In addition, to curb illegal real estate transactions, a real estate registration system was mandatory to ensure the correspondence between the records of the real estate registration and the actual contents of the transaction.

As each government department was dependent on its own documentation measure, however, it was hard to monitor real estate transactions due to an omission or inconsistency of land information records. Another risk of public land administration was corruption because only public officials could access the land information. Lack of accessibility and inaccuracy of land data was the cause of disputes among stakeholders in land transactions, which also affected delaying the implementation of development projects. In this situation, the digitization of geospatial information was necessary to manage the land markets and resolve disputes on land ownership, land administration, and land transaction.

The main goal of the geospatial information system establishment policy is to secure an accurate foundation of land-related data for prompt government administrative work and response to land-related complaints. The system supported the central and local government staff to check land-related data of the development plan comprehensively. In addition, the digitized land management system was built to protect the people's property rights by operating a transparent land system through the disclosure of spatial data. The government also intended to minimize problems, such as speculation and double contracts, by making it easier to check the status of real estate transactions and ownership.

The computerization of cadastral information was promoted since the 1980s in order to identify land ownership and transactions and to manage areas predicted to overheat speculation in advance. At that time, the land cadaster was computerized first due to an insufficient computerization system of cadastral maps and divided management department. The construction of cadaster computerization of 35 million parcels nationwide laid the foundation for the introduction of the Act on the Registration of Real Estate under Actual Titleholder's Name to prevent illegal transactions by registering them in the name of others and enabling end-user-oriented transactions (KRIHS, 2014b). With the introduction of the geospatial information system in Korea in the early 1990s, it became possible to computerize cadastral maps and land-related information, including parcel types, location, and other attribute data.

An attempt was made to enhance the accuracy of the cadastral map because it is the basic data of various subject maps and civil petition documents directly linked to individual property rights. The Ministry of Government Administration and Home Affairs had established a Parcel Based Land Information System that integrates land cadaster (text information) and cadastral maps (figure information), which were the results of former computerized projects. On the other hand, land-related administration took a long time to browse spatial information, attribute data, and legal information. Moreover, to prevent the movement of speculative areas from avoiding regulations, an advanced system was required that could manage land information of individual parcels rather than administrative districts. Accordingly, the Ministry of Construction and Transportation established a land information management system that links various land-related attribute data and legal information based on a serial cadastral map.

In addition to the land policy sector, the demand for a serial cadastral map had increased in various public policy sectors, such as agriculture, forestry, and the environment. The private sector also attempted to utilize the serial cadastral map when establishing development plans for new city development, bridges, and road construction. However, dualization of the Parcel Based Land Information System and the Land Information Management System made it difficult to update quickly and share land status changes on parcel division, merger, and land use plan. The discrepancy between the actual situation and land information can lead to serious land disputes. For example, when the government did not accurately check the land use regulations and granted permission for a development project, the project might be suspended in the future, thereby resulting in enormous damage compensation. The establishment of the Korea Land Information System (KLIS) in 2003 streamlined the management of land-related information and administrative work. The policy achievements of the establishment of the spatial data systems in phases are described below:

- Maximizing the efficiency of the administrative system for limited human resources: Due to dualization of land information registration and management system, budget and manpower were wasted by overlapping work when operating the land registration system or the official land price system. In addition, land information for each administrative department was different, which intensified the conflict of land disputes. In order to solve this problem, overlapping redundant administrative tasks were minimized and limited professional manpower was efficiently deployed.

- Ease of securing public development sites and mitigation of compensation conflicts: Real estate speculation was curbed through the transparency of land transaction information, thereby lowering indiscriminate land price hikes. After the introduction of the pre-planning and post-development systems, the land price soared mainly on the planned development, and the problem of difficulty in securing a development site was improved. In addition, as land price and parcel information become more accurate, the boundaries and prices of the compensation area also became quickly recognizable, thereby reducing the problem of compensation-related disputes and delays in project implementation.
- Enhance the accessibility of information by digitizing land information: The establishment of the KLIS provided the government's administrative services online. Consequently, not only access to information by the public has improved but long-term cost-saving and time-saving effects for handling civil complaints are also apparent at the level of government's administrative management.

Since the 1970s, attempts to curb real estate speculation – such as the officially assessed land price and computerization of land information – have been introduced, creating jobs and producing professional manpower. The training process of land appraisers contributed to improving the discrepancy in land price evaluation of each administrative department so that the official land price system operated smoothly. Moreover, the demand for professionals for the geospatial information system increased due to the computerization of land information and land administration over a long time.

In order to digitize spatial information, the major task was

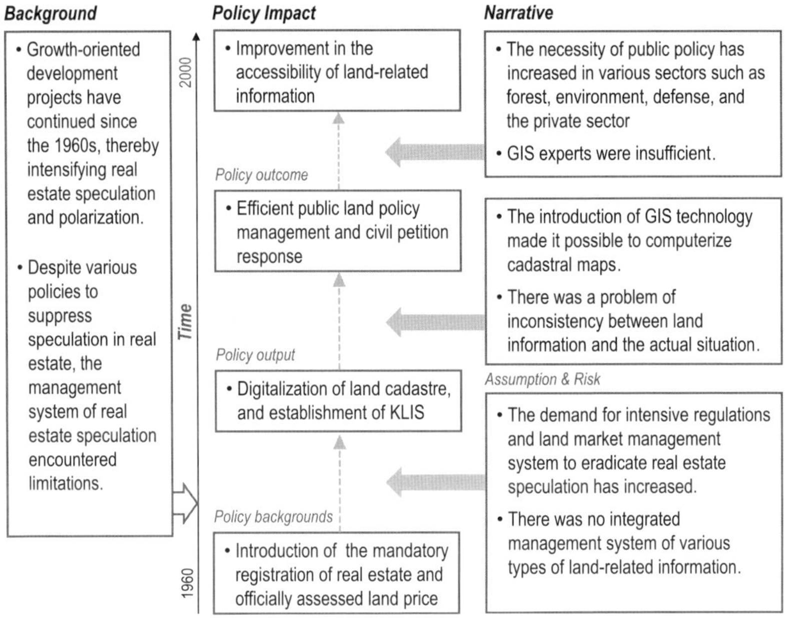

Figure 27. Contribution analysis of managing land markets and digitizing land-related information

to develop integrated systems for the production, management, utilization, and distribution of various types of land information. The difference in the existing work system and data registration method for each administrative department caused the problem of overlapping data or recording the same contents differently in the process of computerizing land information, thereby providing an improvement for the public to overhaul the administrative system. Accordingly, it was possible to establish a more accurate land-related information system through effective land information production and management.

The integrated land information management system was utilized for various civil petitions, shortening service time and enhancing public work productivity, thereby enabling a mature response to potential land disputes. The opening and distribution of spatial information to private companies enabled the expansion of various industrial fields such as transportation and the environment.

It was converted from a supplier-oriented to a consumer-oriented land information management system. However, since the land information was digitized by supplementing the initial paper cadastral map from the Japanese colonial period, there were still problems such as inconsistency with the on-site land condition. Currently, managing ownership of approximately 15 percent of the 37 million land plots in the country remains a challenging issue (The Right Land, 2020b).

CASE STUDY 8

State-of-the-art utilization of a spatial database for smart growth

During the 1960s and 80s, information on cadastral property was inadequate (inaccurate data on residential land units), thereby leading to disputes over land in Korea. Since land management was recognized as an essential factor in the operation and management of the country, the need to manage land information began to emerge in national policy. Thus, efficient land management became possible by introducing the Korean Land Information System (KLIS).

Land conflicts due to insufficient spatial database

Before establishing spatial information, disputes occurred due to land problems (real estate) in Korea. In the first case, Gyeongsan, Gyeongsangbuk-do, the landowner visited the site with a cadastral surveyor to purchase the land, checked the land boundary, and completed the land transaction. However, a dispute broke out with another owner with the ownership of the adjacent land.

In the second case, landowners who bought for speculation on Jeju Island were defrauded by real estate agents. Real estate agents traded the land by defrauding areas where development activities were impossible (areas in conservation green areas or reclamation areas). The real estate agent profited 10 times more than the market price. In the 1990s, when access to land information was limited, people had no choice but to engage in land transactions with real estate agents, which occasionally led to frauds.

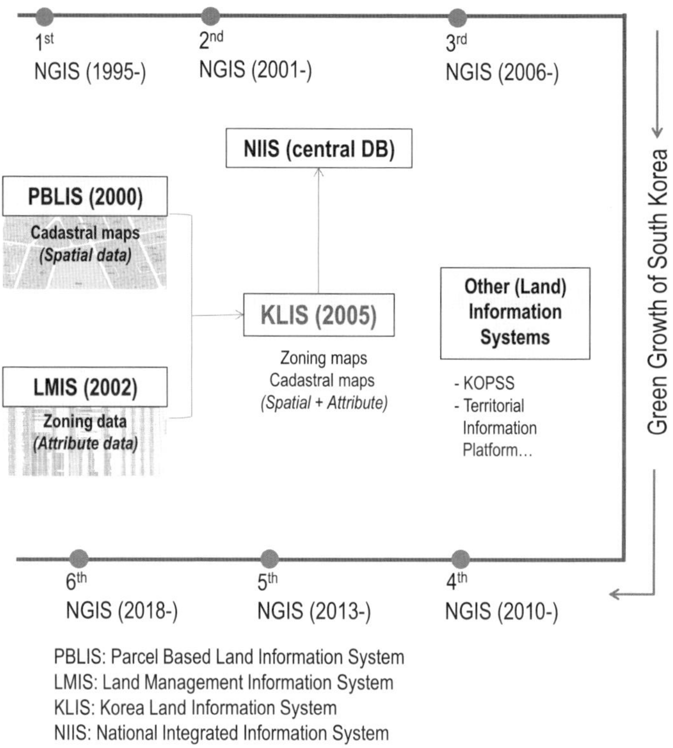

Figure 28. Relationship among systems under the framework of NGIS

Establishment of the KLIS

The Korean Land Spatial Information System (KLSIS) was planned under the National Spatial Information System (NGIS) plan of Korea, which was established in 1995. In the process of computerizing existing land-related information, two systems (PBLIS; Parcel Based Land Information System and LMIS; Land Management Information System) were established. Since the information on the land is dualized, it is necessary to unify the system for the user and efficient management of the land. Consequently, it was integrated into the Korea Land Information System (KLIS) in 2005.

The KLIS is an integrated platform for land policy establishment

Figure 29.
User interface of KLIS (upper) and land use plan detailed in KLIS (lower)
Source: Screen captured on Seoul Real Estate Information Plaza 2021

and land (conflict) management. The platform made it possible to secure basic data for the central government's land policy and establish an accurate land policy. In addition, the local government's land-related department can efficiently perform various land-related tasks and comprehensively manage land-related tasks. It enables the reading and issuance of 13 kinds of civilian documents, such as landuse plans, individual house price confirmation, realtime viewing of land information, and cadastral map. In addition, civil affairs related to 35 types of real estates, such as land transaction permission and real estate development business registration became possible (KRIHS, 2014a). The KLIS is pursuing administrative efficiency and providing convenience to people by establishing a system to handle civil affairs on the

Internet (KLIS website or Government 24 website).

Impact and significance of the KLIS

The effectiveness of the construction of the KLIS was strong. First, the effects on land conflict and administration were significant. The KLIS solved the problem of land disputes by enabling access to information on land. As the cadastral map and land use plan can be easily checked on the Internet, it is possible to accurately check land boundary, land use, and land price. Moreover, the KLIS gives users groundbreaking solutions in land management. It is particularly useful for evidence-based compensation or tax because the price of the land is surveyed annually. The KLIS also provides convenience due to administrative simplification. In the past, landowners had to issue papers for each municipality to find the prices of homes, and for land transactions, citizens had to visit the community service center and file a complaint by fax. With the construction of the KLIS, citizens can receive documents directly on the Internet, simplifying administration. Consequently, it is cost-saving for citizens, as document procedures are reduced; it is also time-saving for government officials to handle complaints.

Second, KLIS is well utilized as the basis for various spatial information systems. KLIS not only contains spatial and property information on land but also continuously links 37 million individual cadastral maps across the country to the KLIS. The connection of national cadastral maps implies that spaces or properties can be compared or analyzed nationwide or by specific regions or cities. Therefore, it is a versatile spatial information system that can integrate national data and be effectively applied to spatial planning assistance. Therefore, KLIS is helpful in resolving land disputes, simplifying administration, and managing individual cadastral maps. If such a land information system were established and applied in developing countries, it would be helpful. In particular, if Korea's KLIS is applied to developing countries, cooperation between the relevant departments of various related ministries and local governments is important; thus, it is necessary to closely examine the characteristics of the cooperative relationship between the central ministries and related departments of the developing country.

Assessment of land management and dispute resolution

As summarized above, various land disputes occurred in Korea after the war, focusing on the demolition of illegal buildings in cities, land ownership, land development and compensation, and real estate speculation. These land conflicts provided an opportunity for Korean society and its urban planning and administrative systems to mature.

The Gwangju Resettlement Town Project was implemented due to the migration policy of the shantytown. The importance of "pre-planning and post-development" was recognized, and systematic urban planning procedures were established. The farmland reform after the Korean War eradicated land monopolies of the landlords and guaranteed individual ownership. After the Farmland Reform, the dissemination of public education quickly spread, which enabled the development of human capital in the industrial society in the future. The Land Readjustment Project contributed to overcoming the country's financial difficulties in the post-war situation and improving the severe housing shortage problem. However, land compensation problems and real estate speculation problems continued to occur during the growth-oriented development era. Moreover, environmental issues caused by urban sprawl also appeared. To preemptively manage the land market, the accuracy and immediacy of land information and related administrative affairs were required. This land conflict has served as an opportunity to establish an integrated Korean land information management system over a decade despite the expenditure of a large budget. The digitization of land information and administrative affairs secured transparency in the land market and increased public responsiveness to potential land disputes.

The resolution of land conflicts has resulted in a substantial positive impact. However, because the land is a fundamental factor directly related to public development and individual property rights, land conflicts continue to arise in many ways in the course of urban growth and development. Even today, various land disputes related to illegal occupation, land transactions, urban development, and land information construction have occurred, and response policies and related systems have been continuously improved.

First, although the government tried to legalize illegal buildings through migration policies and eliminate them in the city proper, the urban poor still remains in cities today. Examining the data on the status of existing illegal buildings in 2019, there remain 26,915 existing illegal houses that were listed on building registers in 1982 or could be identified by aerial photography of that year (Seoul Open Data Plaza, 2019). The government continued to keep it legalized to support the urban poor's living under the Act on Special Measures for the Adjustment of Specific Buildings. The illegal houses have been excluded from the demolition crackdown, and no sanctions have been imposed. This refers to illegal housing that has authorized the right of proprietorship of the residents, taking into account the *de facto* rights of those living by illegally occupying the site. However, such houses could become a target for speculators because the right of proprietorship can be granted to the residents in redevelopment projects. Consequently, the urban poor were forced to be driven to places where they were less protected. Accordingly, the government of Seoul attempted to prevent this by reinforcing the management of the existing illegal housing management ledger and adjusting the trading conditions and related regulations.

Second, as the land market followed the flow of the free market economy, real estate speculation and the privatization of development profits began to repeat. Land and real estate became a means of unearned income and continuously caused problems in the housing supply. To suppress speculation in real estate and stabilize housing prices, policies to suppress demand – such as tax increases and housing supply policies like the expansion of new cities through the discontinuation of the green belt – were implemented. However, in the face of the financial crisis and globalization, regulations and easing policies on the land market were repeated so that the real estate policy was not effective. Recently, to curb a surge in housing prices, regulations have been strengthened by introducing policies such as heavy taxation for multi-homeowners, obligation to live in, and reducing the size of loans.

Third, the Land Readjustment Project – which enabled high-quality urban development at the time of the growth-oriented development – made it difficult to use land inconsistently. The Land Readjustment Project was a business method optimized for efficient land supply. After the site was arranged, the landowner was assigned to use it. Thus, there were numerous cases where the land could not be used as it was intended to. For example, a situation recently arose that impedes urban development by neglecting land instead of constructing buildings to increase land prices. On the other hand, there were cases in which the infrastructure that was installed when the site was created did not fit the building plan. As buildings in the Land Readjustment Project District crossed the age of 20, reconstruction was necessary; moreover, since detached houses were changed to multi-household housing and multi-family housing, there were numerous problems of lack of infrastructure. To solve these problems, various efforts were made, such as promoting the construction of buildings through the Act on Temporary Measures for Promotion of Specific District Development and introducing the Residential Environment Improvement Project. Additional system supplementation is required for previously created sites. However, for the sites to be created in the future, it is necessary to plan the construction of land and the buildings on the ground in the early stages of the Land Readjustment Project.

Fourth, the land information management system continues to have the problem of inconsistency between the actual land condition and spatial data. Since paper cadastral maps written by hand were digitized in the past, inaccurate land information or missing information was registered as it is. When various regulations and urban planning contents are applied to a specific area, the problem of nonconformity among the boundaries between parcels is directly related to the property rights of individuals, which causes land disputes. On the other hand, an omission of land information makes it the government impossible to grasp accurate regulations for the development site. It could occur when the permitted development project has to be brought to a halt, and a massive problem of compensation for damage between the government and private sectors. Accordingly, to increase the accuracy and reliability of land information, the Cadastral Resurvey project is under continuous implementation, and efforts are being made to improve errors.

Korea has grown by resolving a large number of land conflicts. It is important that the government, individuals, and private sector attempt to understand each other's positions in such improvement. Transparency and accessibility of land information have increased due to the development of information technology, but the technology of 'communication', which provides information on situations and interests in the information during the development process, must be improved steadily.

INTERVIEW 1

Approaches to the prevention and resolution of land conflicts in Seoul

In order to draw insights related to resolving land disputes in South Korea, an interview was conducted with Sung Hio Ku, a responsible officer of the Land Management Division of the Seoul Metropolitan Government. He is an expert in cadastral work at the Korea Land and Geospatial Informatix Corporation and the Seoul Metropolitan Government. The following interview was conducted at the Seoul City Hall on May 18, 2020.

Importance of accurate cadastral information to resolve or reduce land conflict

There is a consensus that accurate cadastral maps and ownership information must be utilized transparently in land administration in order to resolve land disputes and appropriate compensation for land, which are issues that underpin the multidimensional facets of the process of urbanization.

One of the definitive measures to sustainably reduce social fragmentation and costs associated with land disputes has been developing data on land plots throughout the entirety of land in South Korea. To that end, paper-based cadastral information that had previously been managed in a fragmented manner became fully digitized and integrated to encompass the management of the entirety of land in South Korea from around the year

Table 1. Cadastral surveying screening

Objective	To secure citizens' land rights and profit
Expected outcomes	• Reducing the social and economic burden of claimants • Providing a quick and easy intervention to recover the infringed rights and interests of the claimants
Time required	90 days per case (including a field survey conducted thrice) in accordance with the statutes
Budget	$4,500 per case on average, which only covers operating expenses (excluding labor costs)
Human resources	Approximately 20 people including private experts, academics, and government officials
Frequency	• 3-4 cases per quarter, approximately 10-14 cases per year • If there is a dispute over the performance of the cadastral survey, the owner, stakeholder, or surveyor shall apply in writing, quarterly review, and a bill and evidence to the autonomous region.
Procedure	1) Submitting a claim letter for cadastral survey screening/examination to autonomous districts 2) Transfer the claim to Seoul Metropolitan Government (Land Management Division) 3) Holding the Local Cadastral Committee for deliberation and resolution 4) Notifying the results to the claimant * In case of re-claim 5) The request transfer to the higher committee (Ministry of Land, Infrastructure and Transport) 6) Review and resolution 7) Notifying the results to the claimant
Others	Review of drawing boundaries and implementing them based on laws and systems

2000 onward. However, the digitization of such vast amounts of information proved to be an enormous challenge, fraught with a wide range of implementation issues. In particular, actual land boundaries and cadastral information that had been digitized were often contradictory. This may lead to issues such as inaccurate assessments and levying of property taxes, causing community disputes, damaging social consensus on principles of property ownership, eroding trust in government, and ultimately exacerbating negative social costs. As such, the establishment of accurate cadastral information associated with ownership rights is of paramount importance.

Conformity assessment of the cadastral survey

Although cadastral data has been thoroughly compiled, civil complaints on inaccurate measurements and errors are continuously being filed. The conformity assessment of the cadastral survey is an attempt to resolve the problems associated with land boundary conflicts. Currently, a large proportion of land disputes received by the Seoul Metropolitan Government comes from the inconsistency between the actual occupancy status and the registered boundaries caused by computerizing the past cadastral map. Prior to computerization, there were fewer complaints due to restrictions like access to information; rather, complaints occurred as erroneous data are computerized and information is released. When this happens, the parties to the land conflict can apply for conformity assessment of the cadastral survey. The dispute resolution is made based on a thorough investigation of the cadastral map and the actual use status, and the details are tabulated below.

Cadastral Resurvey project

In order to prevent land conflicts and to establish a more systematic spatial information system, cadastral reinvestigation projects are underway. The project involves revising or rewriting cadastral records by the real-life boundaries of landowners. In a cadastral reinvestigation project, the purpose is to resolve social disputes caused by inaccurate data. The cadastral maps constructed in the past – including during the Japanese colonial rule – were often inaccurate, thereby resulting in inconsistent registration of cadastral records with the actual status of the land. In response, the Special Act on Cadastral Resurvey was enacted, and the cadastral property research project has been in progress since 2012. The investigation was conducted by combining 100 to 300 parcels considering the required manpower and cost, which takes approximately 2 to 3 years per case. As of May 2020, 1,845 parcels, or approximately 1.2 percent of the total 149,000 parcels in Seoul, were completed. The cadastral map is revised or newly constructed to meet the boundaries of reality. Because of its intense relationship with property rights, more than two-thirds of the residents must agree upon the project. The details are tabulated below.

Efforts to strengthen the importance and capacity of public officials in charge of resolving land conflicts

Conflicts like land boundary inconsistencies often lead to distrust among the public in terms of confidence in the nation, which has failed to accurately measure cadastral conditions rather than conflicts among citizens themselves. Therefore, the role of related officials in charge of this is significant. In order to reduce the negative impact of conflict, officials in charge conduct sufficient consultations with civil servants. In addition, if necessary, public hearings are held to inform the correct facts and collect opinions of residents. In addition, public officials attempt improvement by identifying problems of related laws or systems. The Seoul Metropolitan Government also provides education to improve the professionalism of its representatives. Seoul conducts specialized education classes five times a year for officers of the cadastral division in autonomous districts and holds cadastral survey competitions. In addition, they are educated on capacity building for cadastral civil servants under the supervision of the central government.

Table 2. Cadastral Resurvey project

Objective	To prevent and resolve disputes over land conflicts by providing accurate information after conducting a thorough investigation into inaccurate cadastral studies according to the development of survey technology
Expected outcomes	Establishing a systematic spatial data system and providing consumer-centered spatial data
Period	2-3 years per case by the statutes
Budget	$1,800 per case on average (The municipal budget is drawn up by establishing an implementing plan yearly basis in the autonomous region)
Human resources	Approximately 30 people including private experts, academics, and government officials
Frequency	• Delivering on an annual basis • A combined survey of 100 to 300 lots is implemented in consideration of the required personnel and expenses of the relevant autonomous region.
Procedure	1) Establishing an annual plan by districts 2) Organizing briefing sessions for residents' agreement 3) Conducting field survey/Cadastral resurvey (collection of residents' consents) 4) Implementing boundary adjustment (designated district) 5) Identifying boundaries of the designated district 6) Adjusting and updating cadastral records

Table 3. Training for national cadastral survey in Korea

	HRDC of MOLIT *	LX Education Institute	KASM **	EIRPC ***	Total (Completion rate)
Subject	Cadastral resurvey	Cadastral survey, spatial data management, etc.	The history and future of land register	Administrative practice and capacity building	
2017	80 pers. / 2 units	950 pers. / 26 units	360 pers. / 9 units	185 pers. / 4 units	1,575 pers. / 41 units (95.1%)
2018	80 pers. / 2 units	1,057 pers. / 30 units	120 pers. / 3 units	150 pers. / 3 units	1,407 pers. / 38 units (unknown)

** Human Resource Development Center of the Ministry of Land, Infrastructure and Transport*
*** Korean Association of Spatial Information, Surveying, and Mapping*
**** Evaluation Institute of Regional Public Corporation*
Source: Drawn based on MOLIT 2018b

Linking to future-oriented industries beyond resolving land conflicts

The more financially unsatisfactory, the more the question arises regarding the effect of the national budget input to resolve land boundary disputes such as cadastral investigation. However, since these cadastral projects benefit both the nation and the people, social consensus on the necessity of cadastral projects is necessary. In this sense, the guaranteed protection of property ownership based on actual use is an integral factor in minimizing social damages that may arise from poorly defined property boundaries. In addition, the state cannot only bring about the improvement of the national land administration by constructing accurate spatial information centered on the consumer but also prepare the future society by linking with new industries like autonomous vehicles. In large-scale cadastral projects, it is a field where job creation can be expected as part of a public project.

INTERVIEW 2

Assessing the key effects of Korea's cadaster on inclusive growth

An interview was conducted to identify the impact of Korea's cadaster system on inclusive growth, including the response to land conflict and contribution to environmental preservation. In Korea, a public institution called Korea Land and Geospatial Informatix Corporation (LX) provides support for developing the national spatial information system, the surveying technology, and the cadastral system. John Khan Yun, who works in the Global Business Department (Overseas Expansion Support Center) of LX, was interviewed on May 21, 2020.

A cadaster is a fundamental database necessary to facilitate managing the national land resources. This clarifies the land property right and provides the standards of land value that are used for land transactions and taxation. In developing countries, building the cadaster is one of the most essential processes for effective government administration and future economic development. In the case of Korea, under the colonial rule of Japan, the foundation of the modern cadastral system was established to facilitate the colonial exploitation policy. The cadaster began to be built with several projects including the Land Adjudication Survey Project from 1910 to 1918 and Forest Adjudication Survey Project between 1916 and 1924. One of the needs for building the cadastral system was to clarify the land ownership of the Japanese to extend the influence of the people. At that time, Japan, a colonial power, enacted a number of rules for Japanese land ownership including legalizing land ownership by foreigners, but it was insufficient to guarantee the Japanese right. Another reason was to take control of the property of the Joseon Dynasty. It was necessary to understand the land ownership situation and to clarify the boundaries of the national land. Under these situations, surveying was conducted to collect land information for the entire country.

Land conflict related to land ownership can be resolved based on the cadastral map

In Korea, a boundary land conflict between landowners of

adjoining lands has been previously resolved based on cadastral records. The land conflicts followed by a boundary violation is related to a different land boundary between the information registered in the cadastral map and the area that the landowners actually own. When a land ownership conflict occurs, the cadaster provides legal evidence in preference to the actual boundary, except in the following situations: 1) when the cadastral map is wrongly registered due to technical errors, and 2) when the landowners clearly recognize the difference between the cadastral map and the actual land boundary, and the details are stated in the contract. Under the situation, Korea has implemented the Demarcation Survey for Parcel Boundary, which demarcates the boundary points registered in the cadastral records onto the surface of the land. It is used to define the land boundary with the adjoining lands only when the boundary registered in the cadastral records is clearly true. In order to prevent differences in results according to the surveying method by period, the surveying method has to follow the measurement method at the time of registering the cadastral map.

The Cadastral records support the preservation of environmental asset by providing land information

As the cadastral records play a key role for national development and management, it is also important for environmental preservation. Based on the land information of cadastral records, Korea has efficiently managed land resources. For example, the cadastral map can be a useful tool to manage a development restriction zone called the green belt. The cadastral records provide the overall land information, including land use types, ownership, land value, and facilitating the designation of the development restriction zone. In addition, when the zones are illegally invaded by temporal occupation or construction, a prompt response can be made by checking the cadastral records.

INTERVIEW 3

Korea's experience of constructing spatial information

An interview was conducted to explore Korea's experience of constructing spatial information system. Hyun Hee Joo, who works at the National Geographic Information Institute (NGII), was interviewed on May 22, 2020.

Korea's experience of constructing spatial information

Korea's modernized national basic map includes "Cheonggudo" (1:216,000 scale) produced in 1834 and "Daedongyeojido" (1:162,000 scale) produced in 1861. Subsequently, from 1910 to 1918, the Japanese Government-General of Korea initiated the cadastral survey and 1:50,000 topography maps were produced. After liberation, the national map was modified with aerial photo-measurement technology through the Joint Korea–Netherlands Aerial Photo Project (JKNP) from 1966 to 1974.

JKNP was a project implemented to produce a basic national map with a scale of 1:25,000 by surveying 30,000 square kilometers of land by aerial photographs through technical cooperation between the two countries. The project also supported the provision of mapping equipment and capacity building to carry out aerial photogrammetry projects independently. The project period lasted from August 13, 1966 to December 31, 1969, and a total of $560,000 in aid was provided – which included $200,000 for equipment support, $60,000 for training engineers, and $300,000 for filming, photography, and measuring the reference point.

Computerized maps began to be produced in 1995. Korea is the only country in the world where a digital map of a scale of 1:5,000 has been developed across the entire country. (Developed countries are at the level of 1:10,000 scale). Since then, 1:1000 scale maps were produced for urban areas and the use of maps was diversified, including terrain, information, underground facilities, etc. Since the 2000s, this has changed from individual units to continuous maps. In addition, with the establishment of e-government and National Spatial Data Infrastructure, it is now evolving into a private user-centered map.

Potential and scalability of spatial data

Spatial data is the backbone of national growth and serves as the basis for spatial planning, policy establishment, land administration, environmental preservation, and securing tax revenues. It also provides key information on building major infrastructures, such as roads, railways, ports, etc. as cyber infrastructure of all industries. U-City, Digital Twin, Smart City, and Green New Deal, which are being attempted in Korea in recent years, are all part of the core growth policy that is currently being pursued based on spatial information. Further, the combination of GIS, IT, and BIM technologies are expanding, thereby resolving urban environment problems such as climate change response and fine dust predic-tion.

This implies that the distribution process of spatial data after its collection is more important. It is meaningful only when the information is transparent and distributed in real time. Land conflict and dispute issues also stem from the uncertainty of spatial data. Based on the integrated system of spatial information, Korea has vertically linked the central and local governments and horizontally linked the private utilization systems.

Consequently, the government can reduce data gaps, such as land and real estate administrative information, and make rational decisions on spatial planning, institutionalization, environmental issues, conflict, and securing tax revenue based on location-oriented data. In addition, by disclosing national spatial data to the private sector for free, the spatial information-based service industry, such as mapping services and mobility industries, is continuously expanding.

Implications for developing countries

Officials in developing countries who want to benchmark Korea's experience in building spatial information may already have a good understanding of Korea's system. However, the challenges they still face in the implementation process are 1) the continued interest of the chief policymaker, 2) the preparation of laws and systems, and 3) the organization of dedicated enforcement agencies.

First, Korea achieved the collection of spatial information and rapid economic growth because of the continued interest and will of policymakers. The spatial data produced in the 1960s was reflected in the national territory development plan to construct the Gyeongbu Expressway and to prepare appropriate environmental regulatory guidelines in response to indiscriminate development.

Second, strong laws and systems must be in place to build spatial information in order to have continuous execution, which goes beyond merely the will of policymakers. Korea enacted the so-called Spatial Data three Acts as the largest framework for integrating spatial data – these acts included "the Framework Act on National Spatial Data Infrastructure," "the Act on the Establishment, Management, etc. of Spatial Data," and "the Spatial Data Industry Promotion Act."

Third, it is necessary to establish an executive organization dedicated to spatial data. In Korea, the organization of spatial information policies is systematically divided by business sectors, such as the production, distribution, and standardization of information. The production of spatial information is handled by governments and other related public institutions; the distribution is handled by the National Spatial Information Center, the Spatial Information Industry Promotion Institute and the National Geographic Information Institute; and the standardization is handled by the National Territory Information Policy Officer, the Korea Research Institute for Human Settlements, the National Geographic Information Institute, and the Korean Agency for Technology and Standards.

Chapter 4

LEVERAGING KOREAN EXPERTISE TO INTERNATIONAL CONTEXTS

Promoting land tenure security

Land is a primary asset for households, institutions, and the states, serving as the basis of their livelihoods and a means of production and consumption. In this regard, establishing robust land tenure security protects an individual's rights and an entrepreneur's interests, while minimizing the negative externalities from social conflicts and promoting a vibrant land market economy. Securing land tenure promotes social stability by assuring property rights and means of living, preventing encroachment, and reducing land-related litigation. Moreover, protecting property rights is positively associated with greater investment in the built properties, promoting the formation of an active market for land, and reducing informal land transactions.

A number of developing countries are experiencing difficulties in managing land tenure. When a government's administrative capacity is weak, land tenure is maintained through an informal process rather than through legal means. Moreover, inconsistent management of land results in data inaccuracy, thereby leading to an expensive outcome in registering the land or resolving land conflicts. This emphasizes the role of the government in protecting land ownership and tenure, mediating land conflicts, and ensuring effective management of land uses to pursue the sustained growth of a nation. Thus, it is important for the government to establish a legal framework, which includes plans for regulating land use.

The level of government intervention in land management is

debatable. When the regulations are excessive, the owners' rights on their property can be infringed. Moreover, rigid bureaucratic controls over land can impede the adoption of new industrial activities and creative land use practices. If the land authority is associated with moral hazard, corruption can occur in the process of land acquisition and tax collection. If land-related regulations are rather ambiguous or limited, it is difficult to use the land in an efficient and transparent manner. Therefore, it is crucial to maintain the correct balance between the owners' rights and the degree of government intervention in land use.

While land policies in Korea have evolved through attempting to create a balance between efficiency and equality, the efforts to secure individuals' land ownership and land tenure rights have continued. In the stage of modernization, Korea began recognizing the importance of private land ownership and secured property rights. The right to own and cultivate farmlands was institutionally secured through the Farmland Reform. In the stage of post-war recovery and urbanization, the government attempted to strike a balance between acquiring land for urban development and protecting the property rights of the owner. Thus, the government strived to secure land tenureship on the process of land transactions and compensation.

The individual's property rights were crystallized through the Constitution in 1948. The law established the basis of the capitalistic market economy, protecting the land ownership and allowing for the right of land disposition. The law also states that private property can be limited for public welfare under certain conditions. Thus, it was clarified that land can be expropriated when appropriate compensation is provided. By stating this, the public authority is given to reserve the right to acquire privately owned land to a certain extent for the purpose of public use. Moreover, for land leasing, the Civil Act regulates the extent of the rights of both parties and the lease period mainly to protect land tenants (KRIHS, 1995).

Establishing the data that includes the ownership, price, attributes, and the legal cadaster of land provides basic materials for protecting land tenure. Korea's modern land management system was enforced after the land survey conducted between 1910 and 1918 during the Japanese colonial period, even though it was conducted to exploit the land as part of an imperialistic purpose (LX, 2011). After the nation's liberation, the Cadastral Act was established in 1950. The law provided a basic framework for collecting land-related data, including cadaster, land register, forestry map, and forest land register. This Act enabled appropriate land management based on data and securing an individual's property rights based on pertinent information.

The Land Expropriation Act was enacted in 1962 to secure new land for public development. Based on the Act, numerous public development projects, such as the construction of industrial complexes and expressways, were implemented. However, as the land was acquired through bargaining acquisition in accordance with the Civil Act, compensation measures were occasionally inconsistent. The resultant undervaluing of land caused civil complaints (KRIHS, 2014b). Moreover, there was no measure to exploit unregistered lands or lands without an owner of legal title. In order to overcome the limitation, the Korean government enacted the Special Act concerning the Acquisition of Public Land and Compensation for Loss in 1975. However, due to the confusion with two different standards in the laws, civil complaints and disputes continued. Thus, the laws were subsequently integrated into the Act on Acquisition and Compensation for Land for Public Works Projects in 2002, which is currently in effect.

Based on the legal framework, Korea's land expropriation and compensation systems operate with the publicly notified land pricing and appraisal systems. The two systems set the criteria for officially assessed land prices. The Ministry of Land, Infrastructure and Transport officially announces the price of a standard lot, which forms the basis for publicly notified land price (KRIHS, 2014b). Before the implementation of this system, confusion was frequent due to the difference in the standards of land prices. Evaluating all the lots in the country requires too much time and resources, particularly when it is required to be completed within a short period of time. The price of an individual land is estimated through the Land Price Index Table by the government officials on the basis

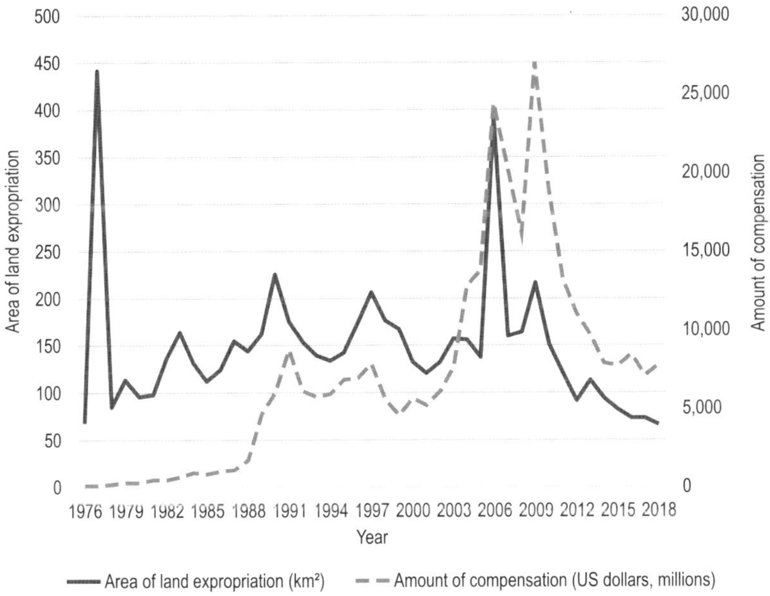

Figure 30. Changes in the area of land expropriation and the amount of compensation (1976-2018)

Source: Drawn based on KRIHS 2014b, 92; MOLIT 2011, 624; MOLIT 2019, 670

Notes: The currency conversion is done based on constant 2021 US$.

of the standard lot price. Moreover, to verify the estimated land pricing, officially certified appraisers evaluate and confirm the price through the public appraiser system.

The Korean government operates the Compensation Council and Land Expropriation Committee to resolve land-related disputes and protect the cases of loss. The Compensation Council can be established under the head of local government to ease civil complaints and mediate conflicting opinions and is mandatory for a certain scale of public projects that covers an area of more than 0.1 square kilometers and involves more than 50 landowners (Article 44 of the Enforcement Decree of the Act on Acquisition and Compensation for Land). The Land Expropriation Committee is an independent administrative office that is expected to be a neutral judge on disputes on compensation between the project operator and landowner and finalize decisions. Thus, the two conflict-mediating systems fully enable the reflection of inhabitants'

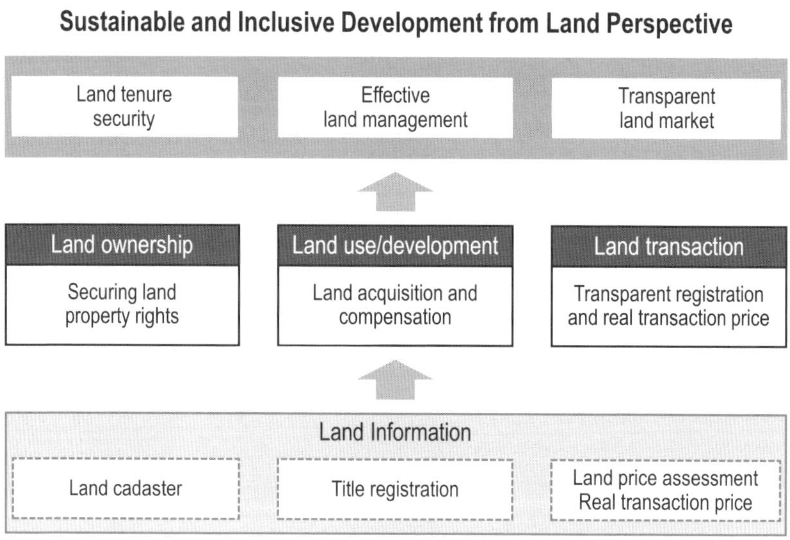

Figure 31. Land administration for sustainable and inclusive growth

opinions and resolve conflicts fairly in a timely manner.

Since the 1990s, the Korean government has strived to increase the transparency of the real estate market. This effort has been concretized by introducing real-name registration for the real estate system and the real estate transaction reporting system. The real-name registration system was implemented in 1995 based on the Act on the Registration of Real Estate under Actual Titleholder's Name to prevent the misuse of title trust for real estate speculation and tax evasion.

During the grace period of a year before implementing the system, approximately 140,000 land titles were transferred to the actual owners (Lee et al., 2014). This indicates that registering a property under a third party who without valid land ownership was prevalent before the system implementation. The introduction of the system contributed to a more transparent operation of the real estate market and preventing speculations by allowing for taxation on the actual owners. Moreover, it is evaluated to have stabilized real estate prices, as speculative demands decreased and real estate transactions were undertaken by actual buyers (Lee et al., 2014).

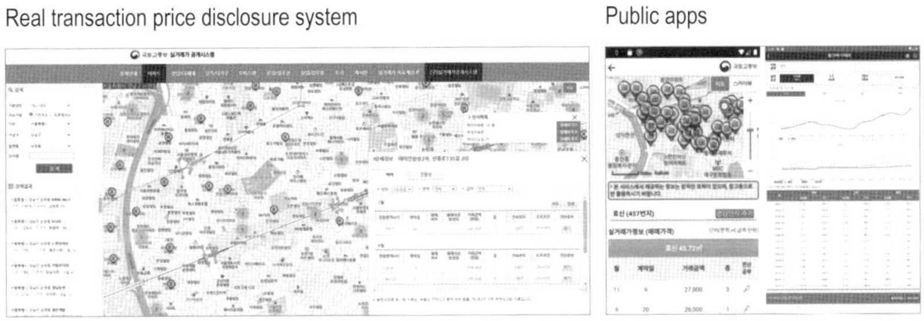

Figure 32. Public website and applications providing real transaction price of real estate

Source: Screen captured on MOLIT 2020; Mobile application by MOLIT; Mobile application by Korea Real Estate Board

The government implemented a real estate transaction reporting system in 2006. The system requires property owners to report the transaction and the actual transaction amount within 60 days of signing the contract. The record can secure the ownership rights and prevent false reporting (e.g., double contracts or under-reporting of the price). This system contributes to fair taxation and transparent transactions as well as developing land and housing policies based on more accurate market prices.

The Real Estate Trade Management System (RTMS) was adopted to effectively manage the reporting system. The construction of the database potentially sorts out false reporting by comparing the transaction amount with the nearby data. The actual price is open to the public, thereby making it possible to be searched using a website and apps provided by public agents. The system contributes not only to improve the transparency of the real estate market, but also to increase the amount of taxation.

In the context of developing countries, setting up the legal and institutional framework for securing land tenure is very important. The framework is critical as the land information will be a basis for public administration and land tenure security. The measures for securing the land tenure must be considered in terms of all aspects, including the process of land acquisition, transaction, reporting, and taxation. Detailed regulations are required to reflect all cases to prevent potential conflicts. When it comes to land expropriation, numerous countries already have the laws on land but do not

INTERVIEW 4

Assessing Korea's land administration policies

Interview and literature reviews were conducted to gain an in-depth understanding of Korea's land administration policies. An interview was conducted with Dr. Mie Oak Chae, who is a former president of the Korea Real Estate Research Institute (KRERI) as well as a former director of the Land and Housing Research Division of the Korea Research Institute for Human Settlements (KRIHS). The interview took place on May 27, 2020. The literature review included her publications on land policy and implementation strategies (KRIHS, 2006) and research papers on land policy changes since Korea's independence (Jung, 1994; Jung, 2010) authored by Dr. Hee Nam Jung.

The establishment of the Cadastral Act and the Farmland Reform: Starting point in granting consistent land tenure rights

The establishment of the Cadastral Act of 1950 and the successful implementation of the Farmland Reform was the basis for secure land tenure in South Korea. The Cadastral Act ensured the establishment of a legal basis for the documentation and management of land registers, land cadaster, forestry cadasters, etc., which are the foundation of land administration in Korea. With regard to the Farmland Reform, there are two significant implications. First, in an agrarian country, the stability of the agricultural population was directly correlated with the socioeconomic stability of the country. In this context, providing a basis for self-reliant livelihoods for those engaged in agriculture was of the utmost importance. Second, within the context of geopolitics, there was a political drive to demonstrate that Korea's economic model based on private property ownership and capitalism was superior to that of the state-centric communist economic model of North Korea. In this regard, although there was some opposition against the Farmland Reform from landowners and certain National Assembly representatives, the government's political will in recognizing the importance of land ownership by a larger number of its citizens proved stronger.

National land use and management policies of the early 1970s: The basis for green growth in South Korea

The policy frameworks established in the 1970s on national land use and protection were central factors in the rapid economic growth and environmentally sustainable development of South Korea. Before the establishment of such policies, there was a period of self-reflection on policies driven purely by economic growth and land development. Such efficiency-driven policies were deemed to incur social, economic, and environmental costs that were relatively high. In response, the following policies were enacted to address these shortcomings.

- Development Restriction Zones (1971): Included in the Urban Planning Act to prevent urban sprawl and protect the natural environment. This was initiated in Seoul before being expanded to the rest of the country
- National Land Planning System (1972): The National Land Planning and Utilization Act to guide large-scale urban development, such as developing an industrial city and conserving rural land.
- Standard Land Appraisal System (1972): This system facilitated appropriate compensation for public development projects and controlled land speculation.
- The Farmland Preservation and Utilization Act (1972): This act laid out the thorough preservation of farmland through comprehensive legislation that governed the conservation of prime farmland from urbanization.
- The Standing Timber Act (1961) and Forestation Policy (1973): This legislature controlled the setup of the registry of timber in the mountains and formed the basis for reforestation projects in forest areas desolated during the Japanese colonial period and the Korean war.

The PPP driven land development of the 1960s and government-led land development of the 1980s: Discussion of their respective strengths and shortcomings

The government was able to expand urban infrastructures, such as housing and roads, in an efficient manner through the

Land Readjustment Projects in the 1960s and 70s. For example, Gangnam, currently the most affluent district in Seoul, was developed through the Land Readjustment Project. However, due to the fact that these projects took a long time to develop land and provide developed land in the market, they proved insufficient in meeting rising housing demands. They resulted in skyrocketing land prices and economic returns being disproportionately concentrated on landowners. As an alternative to this paradigm, the Housing Site Development Promotion Act was promulgated in 1980, with the public sector now taking the lead in land development. Through this Act, large-scale developed land surrounding major cities was supplied, which significantly contributed to resolving housing shortages. However, this method has also been criticized for distorting existing urban planning systems and spatial compositions and causing environmental damage.

The digitalization of land market management policies and related information in the 1990s: Enhancing the transparency and accuracy of land administration

As the world began becoming increasingly globalized in the 1990s, there was a need to increase urban land supply by deregulation and attracting the private sector to urban development. The Korean government determined that land information (such as land ownership and transaction) must be transparent as a policy measure to support this goal. A representative example of this is the implementation of the Real Name Property Ownership System in 1995, which replaced the problematic title registration system. Further, information associated with land transactions would also be registered into a designated information system. These developments ultimately led to the establishment of the Korea Land Information System (KLIS) in the 2000s, thereby resulting in all information on land ownership, land transactions, land use regulation information, and land management being compiled onto one designated system. As such, not only did the KLIS contribute to improving transparency in land administration but it also played an important role in enhancing the accuracy and efficiency of associated administrative processes.

Further, officially assessed land price was introduced in order to provide unified land price standards for various public administ rations, such as tax, charges, compensation, etc., thereby providing increased transparency and more effective regulatory controls on the land market.

The establishment of the National Land Planning and Utilization Act since the 2000s: An eco-friendly national territory management system

By the end of the 1990s, the Urban Planning Act was applied only in urban areas, making it challenging to prevent reckless developments in rural areas. However, in the 2000s, as the Act on the Utilization and Management of the National Territory was incorporated into the National Land Planning and Utilization Act (NLPUA), management systems of rural areas were also implemented. With the adoption of NLPUA, rural areas were able to be managed by urban planning techniques, and development would not be permitted unless an appropriate plan was established first. The NLPUA also introduced several pro-environmental systems, including the Land Suitability Assessment System, Development Permit System, and District Unit Development System, to prevent unplanned development and to protect the natural environment in rural areas.

Land administration policies: A tool to support the economically disadvantaged and foster the middle class, but inconsistent due to periodic changes in philosophies

Korea's land administration policies have been formulated in terms of two aspects. One is to support economic development by supplying urban land smoothly, and the other is to prevent the side effects caused by urbanization, such as speculation and urban sprawl. Such objectives include the development of light industries in the 1960s or the heavy chemicals industry in the 1970s and the large-scale provision of the housing and urban land development system, national land use planning system, and anti-speculation system in the 1980s. Moreover, land administration policies were instrumental in distributing arable farmland to needy farmworkers, and the provision of large amounts of land in a short period was crucial in fostering the growing middle class. Further, a transparent land information system can be said to be another essential policy tool. The Korean government has established a land information system to create market transparency and control the market indirectly rather than having direct regulation since the mid-1990s.

However, land administration policies such as anti-speculation policies were, in certain instances, frequently changed in order to resolve unstable market conditions, thereby resulting in inconsistent policies as well as the erosion of trust among the public. Korea has also experienced the risk of a massive deregulation policy without a spatial plan – for example, the quasi-agricultural area introduced in 1993 to increase land supply by releasing regulation until the end of the 1990s. This deregulation measure contributed to unplanned development that damaged the natural environment of rural areas.

have specific regulations to evaluate the adequate amount for compensation and reach an agreement.

In order to resolve land disputes in developing countries, the government must secure individuals' property based on accurate data, including the parcels managed by customary law. For better land tenure management, having reliable data is fundamental. According to the data form and area coverage of each country, a land survey must be implemented or resurveyed to promote the reliability of land data; for this process, detailed procedures and criteria for solving unmatched information must be prepared and proceed consistently. Moreover, a single representative agency must be designated to collect unified information with the standard criteria.

Further, to reduce the number of land disputes, it is critical to have transparency in the land transaction system. Leveraging the Korean experience of the Act on the Registration of Real Estate under Actual Titleholder's Name and the price reporting system for actual transactions can be helpful. Developing countries must establish their own strategies to report land transactions through a legal process. In order to complete this, it is critical to have a reliable and straightforward registration process to induce bottom-up participation. In addition, the government must regularly manage and update pertinent data. As the system is stabilized, a real-time database can be established, thereby allowing the public to access to land information. Reducing the case of informal land transactions contributes to having more accurate data and protecting the legal rights of the land; moreover, as the government fully understands the market trends, it could provide a better policy for appropriate land management.

Using geospatial information to resolve land disputes

Land information is a critical key source for promoting land policies and improving the efficiency of land management practices. Well-established land information contributes to reducing unnecessary social costs by reducing conflicts, conducting land expropriation, and rational compensation while implementing public projects as well as appropriately managing the land market. The open data platform enables transparent land management and prevents potential corruption associated with land acquisition and transaction.

Land information includes both physical aspects of land such as shape and use and legal information such as registration and tax information. The types of land information and its managing institutions vary depending on the purpose of data collection: managing its physical aspects, registering its ownership and tenure, and imposing taxes. However, it is important to manage them linked and integrated into one platform to increase land administration efficiency and utilization. Land information is managed as a part of geospatial information integrated with various other georeferenced data.

Given that establishing a land information system sets the basis for land management, Korea has exerted a lot of effort to establish the integrated geospatial information system. The country's land administration is operated through two separate systems: the cadastral system and title registration. The basis of land cadaster was completed through the land survey based on the Land Survey Act legislated in 1910.

The foundation of the modernized cadastral system was created by the Cadastral Act enacted in 1950. Through the amendment of the Cadastral Act in 1960, the attribute of cadaster changed from taxation cadaster to legal cadaster. The registers began to

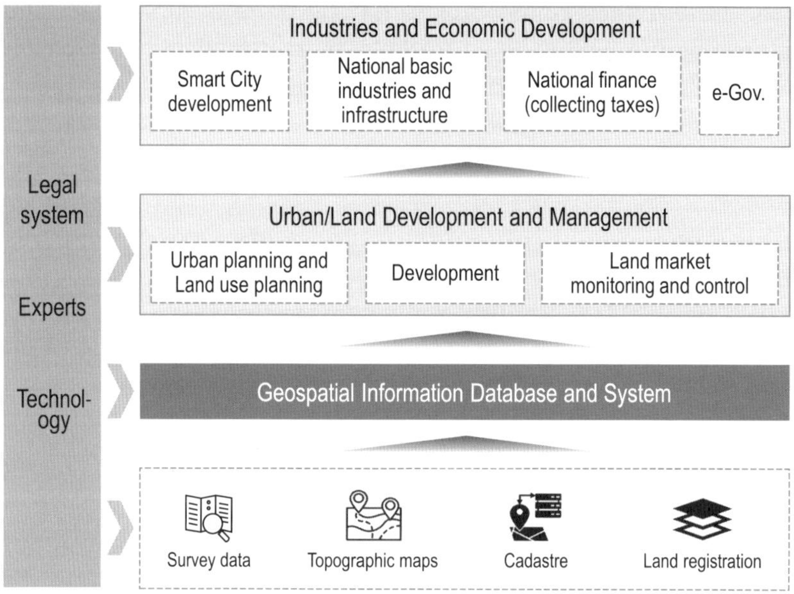

Figure 33. Importance of geospatial information and its impacts

be required to record the location of the land, land category, area, as well as legal owners and shares of ownership. This law was subsequently amended as the Act on Land Survey, Waterway Survey, and Cadastral Records in 2009 to unify survey methods and standards with the management of the cadastral register.

The title registration became organized after the enactment of the Registration of Real Estate Act in 1960. This Act prescribes announcing ownership relations, protecting individual ownership of the real estate, and preventing conflicts in real estate transactions. This Act has been maintained as it is until now.

As land information was initially maintained through a paper-based registry, problems of inaccuracy and non-standardization arose. In order to improve the credibility of the data, the government digitized both title registration and cadaster. Between 1975 and 1985, land books that included all property information were digitized for 34 million parcels nationwide (WBG, 2015). Cadastral maps were also computerized based on a master plan established

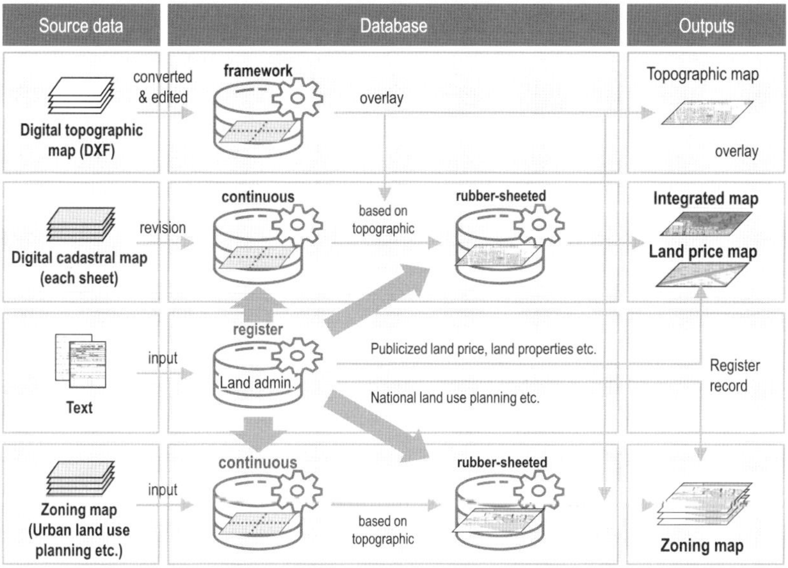

Figure 34. Geospatial DB configuration
Source: Drawn based on KRIHS 2007, 59; KRIHS 2014a, 34

in 1988 (WBG, 2015). Approximately 759,000 cadastral maps were completed in five years between 1999 and 2003 (LX, 2011). More recently, the Cadastral Resurvey project was implemented to correct descriptions inconsistent with the actual land condition since 2012.

As part of the Korean government's efforts to digitize the administrative works, a Five-year Master Plan for National GIS Establishment was enacted in 1995. The goals and sub-projects have evolved in phases: computerizing and organizing land data, constructing a database, connecting and integrating related-geospatial information, and applying the database to various sectors. Through the initiative of the plans, the government could achieve not only the establishment and utilization of major GIS databases but also foster related industries in the private sector and improved accessibility of information to the public.

In order to address the inefficiency due to the incompatible and duplicate land data managed individually by different government organizations, the Korea Land Information System (KLIS) was established in 2004. The KLIS was promoted for three purposes:

Increasing accessibility to information	Improving efficiency in land administration	Establishing evidence-based land policies
• Efficient and easily accessible civil services in issuing administrative documents • Increased data transparency • Fast and accurate administrative process through DB and network	• Cost-savings and better reliability of land admin. through digitalized process • Prevention of duplicate data production and investment by implementing an integrated system	• Real-time identification of land transactions for utilizing policies, such as housing supply, compensation, and anti-speculation • Fact-based taxation policy

Figure 35. Effects of the Land Information System

to streamline land policies and land administration works and to efficiently manage geospatial information; to efficiently carry out various land-related works in local governments and to comprehensively manage land projects; and to complete the creation of standardized seamless cadastral maps (KRIHS, 2014a).

Land information includes various attributes such as real estate registration, geographical features, price, and appraised value, as well as land-related laws and regulations and administrative organizations. The establishment of an integrated data system enables the management of all the different types of data comprehensively; therefore, it could reduce administrative costs and time (KRIHS, 2014c). Moreover, the KLIS improves the quality of civil services from local governments and efficiencies of administrative duties by accessing the data online through the system. People can easily access the data on land use planning and permits, land ownership and tenure, and land prices.

The KLIS has also contributed to evidence-based policy-making. Integrating the data among central and local governments enables more accurate and prompt data. A key factor contributing to the success of this system was the role of local government officials in ensuring the quality of the cadastral maps with online data. The zoning maps and corresponding databases for the 37 million land parcels throughout the country were linked through careful verification by government officials (KRIHS, 2014a).

Establishing a land information system with high data accuracy

CASE STUDY 9

Fixing the mismatch of land boundaries

The cadastral map produced Japanese rule in the 1910s was damaged or deformed after the Korean War, thereby causing numerous errors in the land registration map. Consequently, the location, the boundary, and the area of the land became unclear. The map increasingly became inconsistent due to the dividing and merging of parcels associated with the implementation of development projects (The Right Land, 2020b). Eventually, disputes on land became frequent. It is the background of the Cadastral Resurvey project.

Causes of land boundary mismatch

The causes of land boundary inconsistency are problems with survey reference points, extensive drawing accumulation method, lack of uniformity of survey origin, inaccuracy in recreating cadastral drawings, and errors in the recovery of cadastral maps. The following are the common land boundary mismatch cases: when some areas of the land are duplicated; when adjacent land appears to be separated on the cadastral map; when land is skewed; when there are random errors other than duplication, spaced, and skewing; when there is a locational error while the land form and area are correct; the topographic variation case in which land boundaries have not been maintained due to a complete change in land conditions from the time of registration (Hong, 2011). Currently, approximately 5 million parcels are subject to land boundary mismatch in Korea, which is ap-proximately 15 percent of 37 million parcels (The Right Land, 2020b). Land boundary mismatch has been the cause of land boundary disputes, and land distribution and ownership conflicts continue to occur.

Conflicts due to land boundary mismatch

The land boundary mismatch caused severe land conflict in the area of 267 Yeonhui-dong, Seodaemun-gu, Seoul. 267-10 landowners indicated that part of the land is used as part of the 267-1 (public school site) land. The landowner planned to build a villa on 267-10 land by challenging the landowner 267-1 and clarifying the boundaries. 267-1 land-owner requested to exchange land for doing

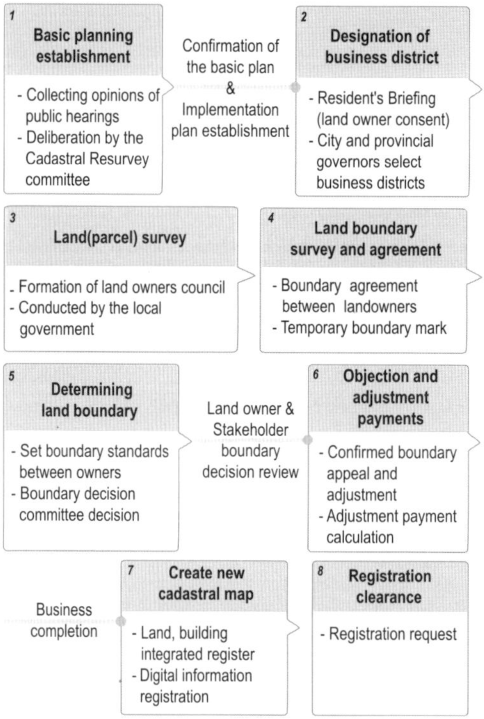

Figure 36. Process of the Cadastral Resurvey project

Source: Drawn based on The Right Land 2021

this correctly. To investigate the boundary of the land, public officials and professional surveying engineers conducted field surveys. As a result of preparing the current status survey and checking the cadastral map, it was confirmed that the boundary lines of adjacent lands overlapped. Land boundaries of 267-10 and 267-1 were marked differently on the cadastral maps created in 1984 and 1993. 267-1 land was marked as 267-10 land as the land boundary was distorted in the course of handwriting. The boundary of the 267 area, which caused severe property rights problems due to inconsistent land boundaries was clarified through the cadastral survey, and the conflict between the residents was resolved.

Cadastral Resurvey project

The Cadastral Resurvey conducted in 2012 identified the problems of current cadastral maps and accurately surveyed the entire land to transform them into digital cadastral maps. This is a project that was implemented to protect property rights and use land efficiently. The Cadastral Resurvey project is carried out by the MOLIT cadastral resurvey planning group. The MOLIT establishes the national Cadastral Resurvey basic plan, and the project implementer establishes the implementation plan. This is a national project that will be implemented until 2030, and the budget required is approximately 15,000 parcels with a budget of approximately one billion dollars. Korea uses the cadastral map, which is the reference point of Tokyo in Japan, and it has a problem of a difference of around 365 meters from the world standard occurs. Therefore, the Cadastral Resurvey was carried out to secure digital cadastral maps by reducing typos and increasing accuracy using a world geodetic system. Through Cadastral Resurvey, social conflicts and land boundary disputes were resolved, and as land boundaries became clear, the value of land use increased. In addition, the digitization

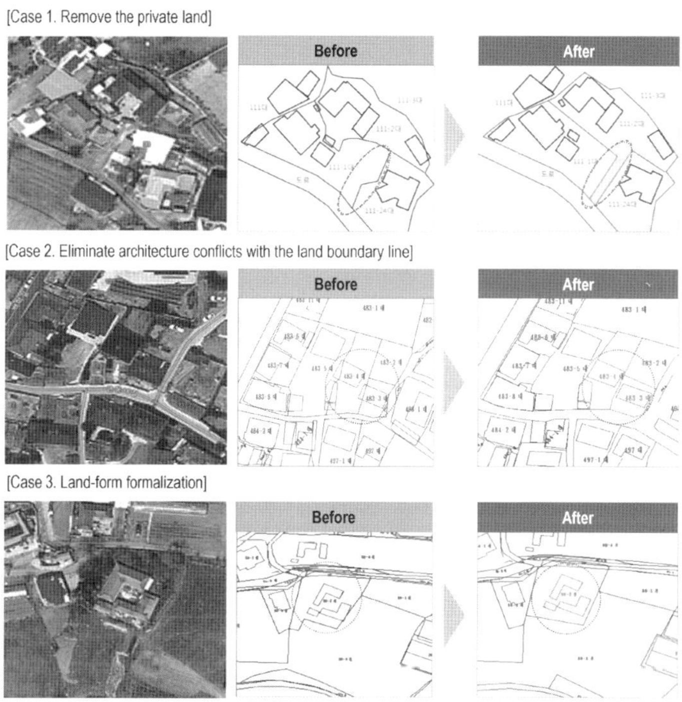

Figure 37. Comparison between before and after of Cadastral Resurvey project

Source: Drawn based on The Right Land 2020a

of cadastral drawings allows owners to check the boundaries of the land, reducing the cost of 75 million dollars per year (The Right Land, 2020b).

The following is the procedure for cadastral reinvestigation. First, the basic plan must be collected through a public hearing and deliberated by the Cadastral Resurvey Committee. Second, the project area is selected through the residents' briefing session, and the city and provincial governors decide the project district. The landowner's consent is obtained through a public hearing. Third, a landowner council is formed to conduct parcel surveys and surveys by local governments. Fourth, a boundary survey is conducted through mediation and agreement between landowners. Fifth, boundary standards between owners are determined through surveying. Finally, objections and adjustments are made through the border decision review between landowners and stakeholders. Consequently, the completion of the project is announced, and the new land and building register are registered as digital information (The Right Land, 2021).

Impact and significance of the Cadastral Resurvey project

The Cadastral Resurvey is implemented using the national budget without burdening residents, and it is characterized by the agreement of landowners. In addition, the task of resolving land conflicts, such as land ownership and boundary disputes, is more efficient because the government is responding to an autonomous region. Through the Cadastral Resurvey, land boundaries can be clarified, social disputes can be resolved, and national property rights can be protected. In addition, it is possible to provide accurate land information by correcting duplicates and inconsistent information and has the advantage of improving administrative services through the construction of digital information. The land boundary mismatch was resolved through the Cadastral Resurvey in Korea, of which three representative cases can be considered. First, land that was not adjacent to the road and, hence, restricted by building permits was adjusted to about the road, increasing its value. Second, land boundaries were clarified for cases where buildings interfered with adjacent land boundaries owned by an another party, which was often a source of severe conflict. Third, when land use was limited due to irregular land forms, the shape of the land was standardized to rectangular forms to increase the usable area and its value.

is crucial for managing land efficiently and protecting land tenure. Numerous developing countries manage land ownership and tenure in a customary manner, thereby leading to the exclusion from the officially managed database. In addition to including the missing data, the digitization of data is required to increase the data accuracy and manage it comprehensively.

Through facilitating advanced technologies and open sources, the government can improve data accuracy at a relatively reasonable cost, and on-site land surveys can also be completed for necessary areas. It is also critical to make an effort to cover the entire country and not exclude vulnerable areas, particularly conflict areas or near borders. For the areas that do not have data that can potentially be subject to land conflicts, a few consistent criteria must be maintained to ensure fairness.

Constructing a measure to officially assess land values is imperative to managing compensation adequately, promoting fairness in taxation, and managing the real estate market. According to the laws of numerous developing countries, the compulsory acquisition of land for public purposes and business purposes is stated, but it does not propose in detail regarding its process and compensation standards for fair and effective acquisition procedures (United States Agency for International Development; USAID, 2013).

The countries can develop standard criteria for assessing the land price, referring to Korea's publicly announced land price system. It provides a land price for referenced lots, which is accessible by all. Based on this data, the price of individual lots is finally fixed through an on-site survey on land characteristics (e.g., physical factors, locational factors, and planning and regulation factors) and an assessment system using a land price index table. Releasing this information to the public and increasing accessibility online contribute to enhanced transparency and fairness in imposing taxes and development charges, providing compensation. Later, the system can be further developed to also keep track of real transaction prices. This system should be developed as a part of the land administrative data system.

After constructing the digitized land data and data of assessed land price, the integrated land administrative system should be

INTERVIEW 5

Exploring Korea's geospatial information system and its implications

In order to deeply analyze the success and failure factors of Korea's geospatial information system and its applicable lessons for developing countries, the interview was conducted with the eminent professional in the GIS sector in Korea. The interviewee was Dr. Hosang Sakong, who is currently a Director-general of the National Geographic Information Institute and a former director of the GIS Research Division and Global Development Partnership Center at KRIHS. The interview took place on May 20, 2020.

Korea's geospatial information system

Korea has developed its geospatial information system, including land information system, in a relatively short period based on a concrete development framework and supporting factors (organization, human and financial resources, etc.).

Korea's geospatial information system could have developed successfully with the government's strong willpower, secured financial resources, supporting legal system, ICT and urban sector's human power, and favorable IT infrastructure. However, the intense efforts by the central government resulted in the passive participation of local governments, and it led to the low utilization of the system in the local environment.

Drawing the lessons from Korea's case, the following factors must be emphasized to successfully establish a geospatial information system, which includes a land information system in developing countries. First, an overall long-term plan and an implementation plan by each phase must be developed in the beginning stage, while considering the country's economic scale and IT infrastructure status. The plan must include a longstanding vision and standardization measures considering that the expansion of the data system to increase its efficiency and prevent the sunk cost. Second, the laws and regulations that are to support the facilitation of the system and DB for administration must be well-established. Third, an effective governance system must be implemented, as geospatial information includes information on various sectors. A well-integrated communication system among related sectors, as well as between central and local governments, is required for effective data management. Finally, supporting manpower with skilled and experienced experts is critical to continuously advance its system.

Implications for developing countries

While applying Korea's development cases in developing countries, the following aspects must be emphasized: understanding the infrastructure status and capacity of countries, developing a management plan, and strengthening the professional manpower. While implementing the GIS system in a target country, it is critical to establish an adequate plan for the country's economic status and infrastructure level. The project level can be designed based on the following categories: i) installing Geodetic Control Point (GCP) and mapping (cadaster, topographic maps, etc.), ii) implementing spatial information DB and developing application systems, iii) integrating related geospatial information systems, and iv) implementing smart services related to ICT. Moreover, not only establishing its data system but also strategies for management and utilization of the system must be emphasized. If the DB is not regularly updated and managed, it will lose its credibility; thus, it is essential to designate the organization in charge and manage it adequately and comprehensively. In this respect, Official Development Assistance (ODA) institutions are recommended to also implement follow-up projects for system management and evaluation of the system's usage, as numerous developing countries struggle with its weak capacity of management of the system. Lastly, it is pivotal to train professionals in the related sectors to effectively manage and further develop the system. As an example, an education center for urban planning and geospatial information in Uzbekistan, founded through a KOICA-funded project, has assumed an important role in educating GIS professionals. It operates various courses from two to three weeks to a one-year course for specialists, government officials, and young professionals.

Appropriate technology for developing countries

For effective management of the system, appropriate technology must be considered for developing countries. In contrast, countries in a development stage can consider the measures to construct the spatial data system that economically facilitates the use of appropriate technology. For spatial data, archived high-resolution satellite images and images taken by drones as well as open street maps, thereby fully utilizing open data sources. Aerial photos and drone images can also be utilized to manage informal land occupation and construction of illegal buildings and structures. For administrative data, it can be formed through easily managed and relatively cost-efficient programs. Moreover, open source-based general-purpose software must be facilitated for saving the costs and increasing application and implementation.

developed. Integrating the data that are operated and managed by different governments contributes to increasing the efficiency of land administration, modernizing the administrative process, and improving accuracy, therefore reducing land disputes. It brings economic benefits as well.

The countries' governments must design a database system based on a comprehensive legal framework and regulation, involving all land-related institutions. It must also contain the measures of data standardization considering further data integration and extension. The system must be developed while considering the government's capacity not only of establishing the system but managing and operating it. It is critical to manage and update the data system regularly not to lose credibility, so it must be expanded by stages. The role of local governments and having a closely coordinated system between the local and central governments must be emphasized, as local governments will mainly utilize and manage the data system.

Applying geospatial information to effective land/urban management and policymaking

Active and widespread utilization of geospatial information is a critical tool to ensure that limited land and ecological resources are effectively managed, which, in turn, is a key driver of long-term sustainable development. In this regard, the KLIS provides an example of how geospatial information may be utilized to resolve land disputes. With systems like the KLIS, the scope of spatial information may be tailored by areas (e.g., nationwide land, specific urban areas, etc.) depending on the objectives. Moreover, integration with ITS and the deployment of the big data technology may be valuable in supporting evidence-based spatial planning and analysis, which in turn may be utilized in national/urban policymaking, the delivery of public services including support for vulnerable social groups, and job creation in related industries. In particular, establishing an effective spatial planning analysis system is an essential tool that can enhance the value and efficiency of land usage through the integrated analysis of infrastructure and land use planning. Moreover, for countries and governments operating under financial and infrastructural constraints, spatial information provides an invaluable asset for maximizing socioeconomic growth potential with minimal time, financial, and energy inputs. The specific benefits of spatial information may be distilled into the following four categories:

- The establishment and utilization of a supporting system for national/urban spatial planning
- Integrated urban management services including support for vulnerable social stratum
- Job creation and industrial growth
- Key infrastructure for green growth

With the objective of establishing and operationalizing a digitized land information, Korea has been actively developing a national spatial information framework and utilization strategies. A key factor to consider about using geospatial information is that detailed implementation tasks must be executed by phases every three to five years, with planning that reflects current and projected needs. Through these processes, South Korea has developed and utilized highly robust national and urban management models and delivered convenient and impactful public services for its citizens. Further, Korea was able to foster human capacity in information technology, and from 2009 onward, green growth policies were directly linked to national development strategies (Green Growth Committee of Korea, 2009).

The establishment of a national/urban spatial planning model through the National Korea Planning Support System (KOPSS) and Virtual Seoul

The launch of the NGIS project in 1995 heralded not only the establishment of a land administration system as well as the planning for the development of a more multidimensional analysis system. As a result of this momentum, the KOPSS was developed and launched in 2006 (KRIHS, 2014e). The KOPSS was a tool for scientific land planning and analysis based on geospatial information. The central government and local authorities could utilize the system to diagnose urban spaces and simulate development interventions, ultimately supporting evidence-based urban planning policies. For example, the system can be used to assess where in the city certain types of infrastructure or facilities are lacking, and prioritize investments accordingly. Further, the development of this system was led by the national government and diffused through local governments, thereby avoiding replicated efforts resulting in many similar systems. From its onset, the system was able to be seamlessly utilized by both central and local governments. The system comprised the following five modules (KRIHS, 2014e) and was in use until 2016. Currently, a new system is being developed that incorporates the functionalities of KOPSS.

- Urban infrastructure planning support module
- Land use planning support module
- Regional planning support module
- City maintenance planning support module
- Landscape planning support module

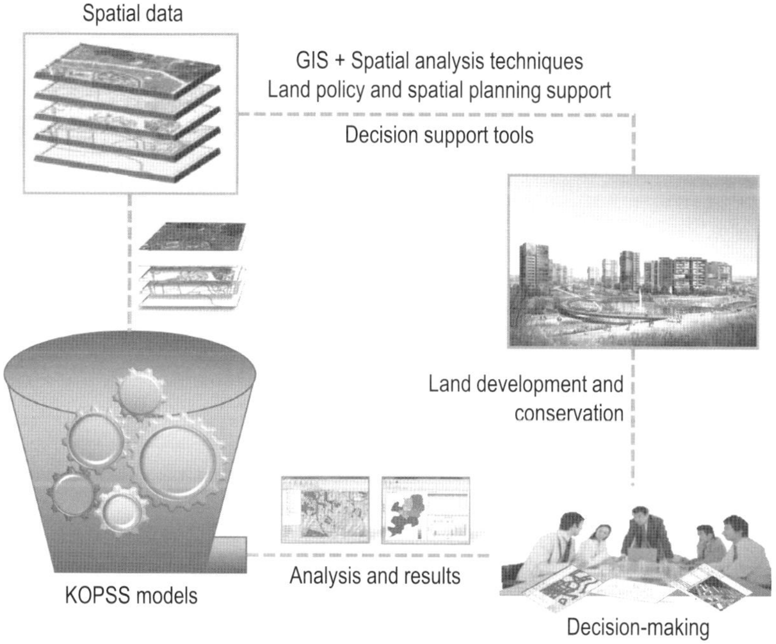

Figure 38. The concept of KOPSS as a tool to support policy decisions
Source: Drawn based on KRIHS 2014e, 10

Virtual Seoul was developed in 2019 as a 3D digital twin of Seoul, where the user can explore the entirety of Seoul's above-ground environment in a virtual space. The greatest utility of Virtual Seoul is that it enables the integration of extensive sources of data, such as traffic volume, demographics, environmental and architectural data (i.e., building and architectural designs for new remodeling/redevelopment projects) in order to simulate the effects of various types of urban interventions (Seoul Metropolitan Government, 2021b). In this sense, Virtual Seoul represents an important tool to preemptively control developments that are not aligned with Seoul's urban development strategies. And this system simultaneously supports evidence-based policymaking processes on key issues such as managing atmospheric pollution and heat islands. Currently, the Seoul Metropolitan Government is interlinking information integrated into Virtual Seoul, such as internal spatial information for public buildings and subway stations with other databases to further enhance the value of the system.

Seoul Transport Operation and Information Service (TOPIS): Control tower of integrated urban management, a platform for collecting and utilizing urban data

Seoul's TOPIS provides a notable example of how a wide array of geospatial-based data can be leveraged to manage urban operations in an integrated fashion. Through a network of numerous CCTVs linked to the platform, urban spaces in the city of Seoul are monitored round the clock, and urban transit, disaster

Figure 39. The interface of 3D-based Virtual Seoul (upper) and simulation of environmental changes (lower)

Source: Screen captured on Seoul Metropolitan Government 2021a; Seoul Metropolitan Government 2021b

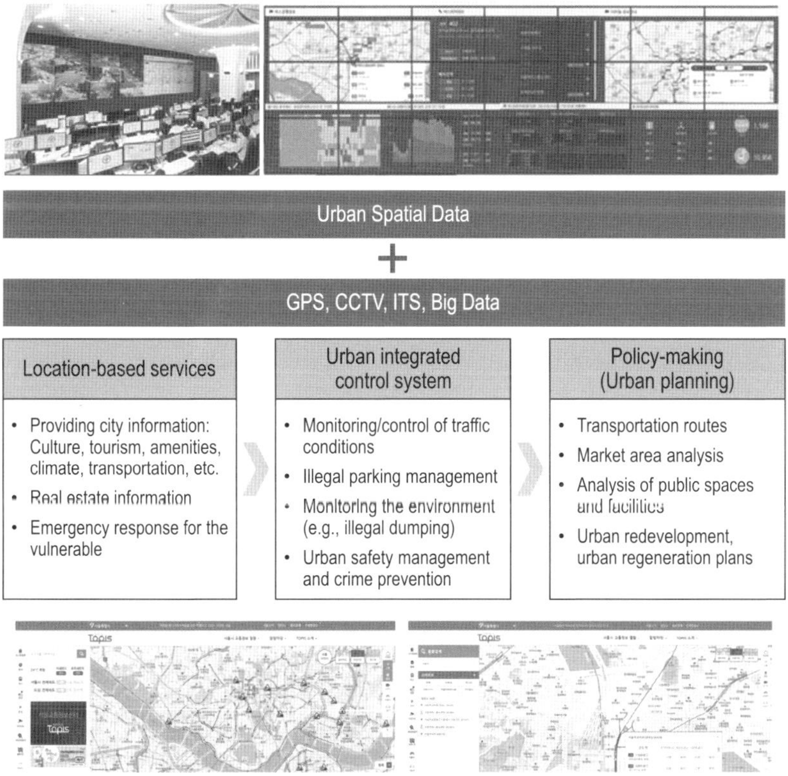

Figure 40. Seoul TOPIS: A case of urban management and policy establishment using urban spatial data

Source: Drawn based on Lee 2014; Screen captured on Seoul TOPIS 2020

risk management, and urban security functions are implemented in a seamlessly integrated manner (Lee, 2014). In terms of support for vulnerable social groups, a few examples include the detection of irregularities in the movement of the physically disabled via sensor technology that is automatically linked to emergency response services. Another example is the integration of GPS with fire detectors in dilapidated areas of the city, thereby enabling the rapid dispatch and coordination of first responders. Moreover, the enormous amounts of data being continuously collected through TOPIS are systematically analyzed and utilized for data-driven policy-making, including the planning and implementing urban development and regeneration programs. The following are a few implications of an urban management system based on geospatial information: First, although it was initially developed with only relatively rudimentary services, the functionalities and the added value of TOPIS were gradually augmented over the past 20 years in alignment with public needs and available resources. Consequently, the TOPIS system currently comprises six interlinked primary platforms capable of operating independently (Lee, 2014). Another implication is the institutional cooperation structure that has been established to enable data sharing. As a case in point, CCTVs monitoring central locations in Seoul are typically managed by the Seoul Metropolitan Police Agency. Before the current iteration of TOPIS, the Metropolitan Police Agency was highly reluctant to share related data and information. However, through continuous consultations with the Metropolitan Police Agency (Seoul Metropolitan Facilities Management Corporation; SMFMC, 2020), the Seoul Metropolitan Government managed to establish a practical spatial information sharing framework from 2001 onward. This governance not only contributed to reducing the operational budget but was also a critical component for collecting accurate data for data-based transportation and urban policies.

The creation of an industrial ecosystem through job creation and industrial expansion

The development and utilization of geospatial information systems can contribute to creating new jobs and a new industrial ecosystem. In South Korea, the development of the national geospatial information system was considered one of many initiatives to fundamentally transition toward a knowledge-based society. Through the project, key sectoral and technical specialists were fostered, and they expanded their expertise to the academia, the public, and the private sectors. As these specialists continued to manage land administration tasks such as land surveying, database and software development, and the distribution of data, the scope of their work continued to expand in alignment with national priorities, thereby leading to the creation of new jobs. Further, the

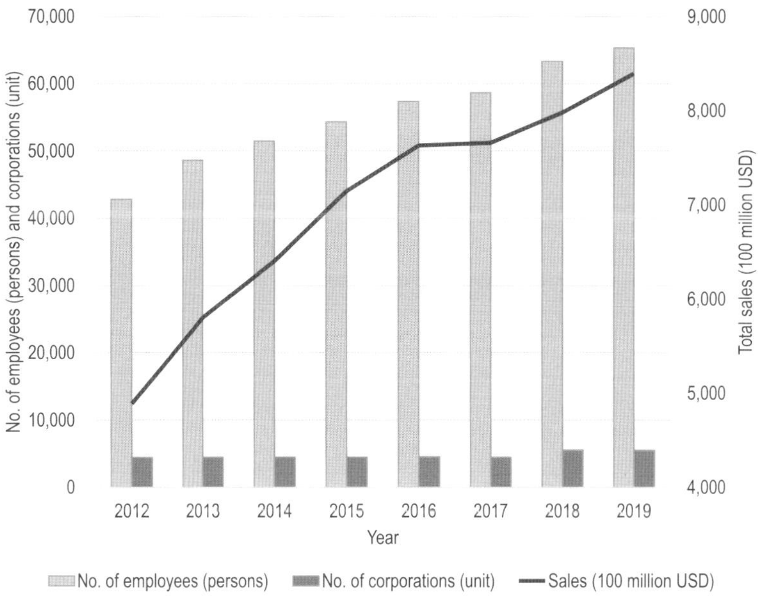

Figure 41. Changes in the Korean spatial information industry (2012-2019)

Source: Drawn based on MOLIT 2021

Note: Since the survey of the spatial information industry in 2012, annual sales have steadily increased to 10.2%, 7.5% of workers, and 3.5% of corporations.

government has also implemented tax incentives for companies in relevant industries and actively supported various pilot projects, thereby further facilitating the growth of the private sector. Such programs also went beyond targeting only technical experts. For example, in the midst of Korea's financial crisis of the 1990s, the national government pursued projects like the "Digitization of Underground Infrastructure" that engaged job seekers and the unemployed (KRIHS, 2014a). The project provided basic training for those without the expertise and deployed them as survey personnel. Thousands of people accessed gained employment opportunities through the project, providing valuable support for establishing the geospatial information of Korea.

One aspect worth highlighting with regard to the development of an industrial ecosystem is that investments in the geospatial information industry tend to lead to more excellent job creation effects than other areas. For example, when the government invested $800,000 in geospatial information industry, it led to the creation of 31 new jobs, a rate that is, on average, 1.5 times higher than the job creation effects from other program investments (Korea Labor Institute; KLI, 2014). From 2012 to 2019, the annual average increase in workers in the geospatial information industry was 7.5 percent (MOLIT, 2021).

Key infrastructure for green growth

When environmental pollution and the erosion of natural resources outpace growth from industrialization and urbanization, the pursuit of economic growth is rendered meaningless. Although Korea endeavored to protect farmland and forested areas, it struggled with high environmental and social costs arising from rapid industrialization and urbanization. In this context, the Korean government assessed that green growth would be possible when national geospatial information converged with green technology throughout the public sector, private sector, and individuals and becomes a ubiquitous aspect of economic and social activities (Joint Ministries of Korea, 2014). To this end, the Territorial Information Platform was developed in order to digitally manage the entirety of digital spatial information and paper maps produced in Korea while ensuring that relevant data is widely accessible and utilized. Through this platform, the public and private sectors, and individuals have access to comprehensive spatial information including those based on map coordinates and satellite imagery free of charge or at a nominal fee. Moreover, as the platform includes built-in spatial analysis functions, even those without specialist knowledge can utilize spatial data easily (NGII, 2021).

This information can be integrated with topographical, transport, agriculture and forestry, water, geological, and cultural asset data. Moreover, through interlinkages with technologies related to energy/resource consumption, emissions reduction, renewable energy, etc., geospatial information currently represents a basis for the environmentally sustainable development and usage of national land. For example, response scenarios and models to minimize human and material losses in natural disasters are being formulated

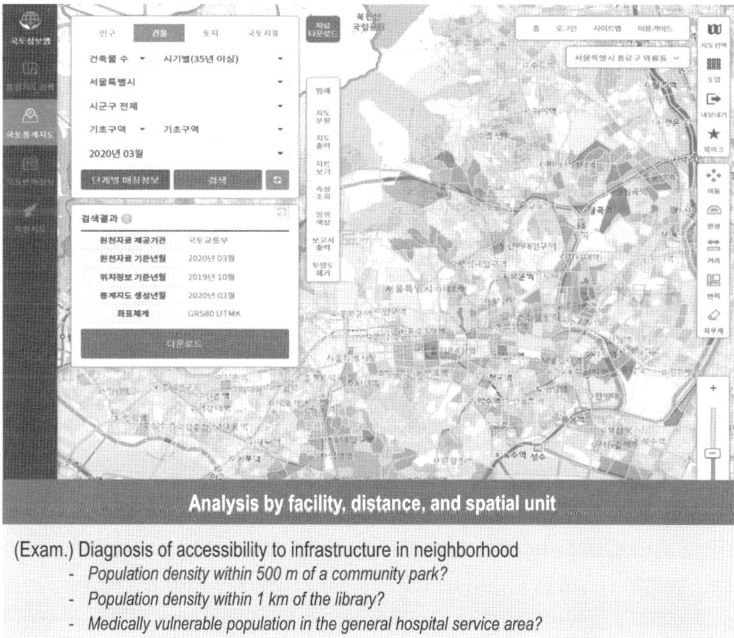

Figure 42. Web-based spatial analysis tool provided by the Territorial Information Platform

Source: Screen captured on National Geographic Information Service 2020

with geospatial information integrated into water and forestry management processes.

A critical factor in the effective utilization of spatial information is the phased implementation of short- and long-term planning that takes the maturity of spatial information and ICT/communications infrastructure into account. Further, the objectives of the plans in each phase must be aligned with addressing the most pressing challenges in land administration or urban management. For example, in the case of South Korea's national information system development, the specific objective was to develop an integrated database for previously fragmented land plot information and each phase of development considered the capacity of existing telecommunications networks (KRIHS, 2014a). The issues related to cost requirements can be addressed in two ways. First, leveraging disruptive technologies can mitigate the high costs associated with traditional methodologies of establishing spatial information. For example, drones can be utilized in place of aerial photography to generate spatial data. Second, open-source data such as archived aerial photographs combined with open street maps can offer ways to obtain spatial data free of charge or at minimal costs.

With regard to data-driven urban services and management, not all cities may be able to develop and deliver highly advanced systems and services from the beginning. Such systems and services must be developed in a manner that takes into account the maturity of the technical and economic development environment, and gradually improved upon.

In the initial stages, it is necessary to provide comprehensive location-based information across a wide array of sectors through various mediums to ensure equity and transparency in the provision of public information. Such sectors may include transportation, culture, tourism, convenience facilities, climate, environment, etc. As information provision frameworks and channels mature, they can then be scaled up to encompass integrated urban diagnosis, management, and problem-solving functions. This may include enforcement of regulations on illegal parking and littering as well as general crime prevention. Finally, once sufficient amounts of data, expertise, and functions are accumulated, data can be routinely analyzed to provide an objective and accurate basis for urban development, urban regeneration, and public transportation planning. In tandem, highly impactful services to support vulnerable social groups may be delivered cost-effectively. For example, sensors with GPS functionalities to support and manage crime prevention, disaster management, and ambulance dispatch can be implemented at a relatively low cost.

The creation of jobs that utilize geospatial information is fundamentally based on the development of a wider industrial ecosystem. This factor has profound implications for a country's internal human capital and capacity to identify and resolve urban challenges in a sustainable manner. To achieve this, appropriate goal-setting and implementation planning by phases are necessary.

- Phase 1: Capacity building and training for specialist expertise

Figure 43. Spatial data for green growth

centered on database development.

- Phase 2: Supporting the private sector and fostering new industries such as software development, systems development, research and education on information dissemination, etc.
- Phase 3: Identifying and operationalizing pilot cities or services in order to engage the private sector and determine specific public sector needs.
- Phase 4: Expanding usage and export of technical expertise and products.

A country's sustained growth may be achieved when the active utilization of spatial information for socioeconomic activities proliferates from the public sector to the private sector and, ultimately, to individuals. This is because the utilization of spatial information across all segments of society can further stimulate land use as an economic growth engine while considering energy and cost-effective resource management and environmental conservation.

In this regard, two factors must be accounted for in order to induce a paradigm shift toward green growth. First, the opening and interlinkage of geospatial information must be backed and supported by policy. In other words, there must be a high level of awareness of the importance of the utilization of geospatial data in the central government in order to facilitate sustainable urban and land development. Second, there must be the development of and investment in green technologies. Accordingly, investments must be made to develop priority green technology and application systems that address the specific challenges of a given country.

Building green growth initiatives for action plans

Numerous developing economies often face complex challenges, typically including an overreliance on inflexible or anachronous decision-making processes and a lack of spatial information infrastructure. In this context, the establishment of green growth initiatives must be underpinned by institutionalizing of a body that manages land disputes and leads the formulation of sustainable and inclusive growth policies. Through such an institution, the government will provide active leadership and initiative for effective dispute resolution, stakeholder management, sustainable growth in land administration, and spatial planning. In particular, such institutions enable governments to establish clear policy frameworks and project prioritization mechanisms, which facilitate more proactive and preemptive approaches to resolving potential land ownership and management issues and can lead to the development of systems and services for the vulnerable. Moreover, ensuring that open discourse on land ownership/management issues arising from industrialization and urbanization occurs through such a public consultative body will likely strengthen transparency and trust in government policy.

In addition, monitoring projects and communicating with

Figure 44. Organizing green growth initiatives

local users (citizens) are essential for establishing governance. This can be confirmed by Korea's push for establishing a spatial information system throughout the first to sixth national spatial information plan and its emphasis on building a demand-oriented system by experiencing the limitations of a supplier-oriented system (MOLIT, 2018a). By preparing a system that collects and reflects feedback from the users, the spatial information can be developed and utilized to meet the needs of users and their priorities when constructing the system and infrastructure related to spatial data. Accordingly, the state will protect the property rights of the people and adequately perform its public role and provide appropriate protection, particularly to socially vulnerable groups, by setting aside a specific budget.

As good governance for sustained growth is an ever-evolving concept, it is not sufficient to simply establish an organization;

its structures and operational frameworks must continuously be updated to reflect changing contexts. The development of Korea's inclusive growth governance model illustrates the importance of maintaining a flexible approach to governance and represents the merging of spatial and economic policies through the establishment of spatial information and related systems. Korea's model for green growth governance can be summarized in the following three characteristics:

- The development of sustainable national geospatial planning and spatial information
- Utilization of spatial data to improve quality of life and enhance national competitiveness
- Central government-local government-private sector collaboration through a dedicated institution

In the early stage, Korea's model for inclusive growth governance proved to be instrumental in establishing frameworks for land management and spatial information management for dispute resolution and efficient usage of land in a highly vulnerable post-war environment. Going beyond dispute resolution, Korea established social balance and order through governance. This governance model was also instrumental in creating new growth engines for national economic development, such as the development, opening, linkage, and convergence of spatial information (Green Growth Committee of Korea, 2009). However, there were demands for policies that could be tangible at the local level after the development of national policy and the construction of infrastructure. After the concentrated growth in the metropolitan area and the implementation of its deterrence policy, problems arose in local areas with the weakening of self-reliance in the provinces, the reduction of the local population, and the increase in unemployment. Consequently, changes to governance structures were also made in which regional development policies were pursued. Further, the Presidential Committee for Balanced National Development is a representative organization established in 2003 (Presidential Committee for

Balanced National Development; PCBND, 2021). Under this system, local development and investment were carried out through the division of the central and local government roles as well as the utilization of private capital to revitalize the local economy.

In order to support economic development through inclusive growth in such a manner, Korea also instituted a body similar to an initiative specifically to coordinate a systematic framework for collaboration among the central government, local government, and the private sector, with clearly defined roles (Joint Ministries of Korea, 2019).

For relevant governance frameworks to be sustainable and scalable in developing countries, central government strategies and plans must be operationalized with specific functions and tasks through local government cooperation and private sector participation. Effective public-private collaboration structures also provide inclusive growth governance frameworks with the appropriate tools to objectively assess and improve public policy. Therefore, proper vertical (clear and logical distinction of roles and responsibilities among stakeholder groups) and horizontal (full and equal participation among stakeholder groups) balance among the central government, local government, and private sector are required for an impactful and sustainable growth ecosystem to be formed.

Institutionalization of a central government consultative body for inter-ministerial coordination

A consultative body under the authority of the central government composed of relevant ministries will ensure that policy and implementation processes are consistent and able to comprehensively reflect key sectorial issues. A mechanism must also be put in place to gather input and advisory from external research institutions and private sector industrial expertise to ensure that the technical accuracy of policies is thoroughly vetted. Moreover, a comprehensive and well-coordinated governance framework provides an integrated mechanism for reexamining and refining inclusive growth strategies, identifying sectoral outcomes, and establishing detailed implementation plans. Integrating these factors with national development strategies will likely ensure that growth and development are sustainable and inclusive.

Cooperation among developing countries and with the broader international community

In light of material and technical limitations that may constrain unilateral efforts to resolve land management challenges, it may be more effective in certain instances to pursue cooperation with the international community. Opportunities to leverage knowledge and experiences from similarly affected countries and advanced economies may provide valuable technical and policy insights in such efforts. Further, material and financial support for establishing inclusive growth governance frameworks may also be accessed from the international community, such as international development organizations and partner governments. In such instances, a green growth initiative can function as a channel for communication and engagement with the broader global community.

Interaction between private and public authorities

In order to achieve inclusive growth, active intervention by the central government is inevitable. In addition, local governments play a major role in determining the architecture, scope, and nature of public service delivery aligned with the needs of the most vulnerable segments of society for a given area. Accordingly, a clear distinction of roles must be made with the central government leading the formulation of pro-poor policies and related projects and local governments with more specific regional/local information responsible for implementing them.

In addition, it is crucial to formulate a public-private cooperation framework to improve technology development and service quality (supporting vulnerable segments of society using spatial information) through continuous feedback and monitoring of target groups and stakeholders. Such a framework will likely have noticeable positive impacts on developing effective governance structures and the advancement of inclusive growth.

Strengthening the capacity of government, experts, and citizens

To establish, utilize, and manage land and geospatial information system, it requires a high volume of professionals specialized in geospatial technologies as well as the creation of public awareness of land administration and GIS systems and their utilization. Strengthening professionals' manpower will contribute not only to operate the system but also to promote the technological competitiveness of a nation and the development of relevant industries. Further, it is crucial to improve the capacity of vulnerable populations, as they suffer from land disputes due to a lack of awareness of their rights and the land administration system.

In order to promote the effective operation and management of the geodata information system, Korea has included strategies for cultivating human resources and fostering the related industries as a part of National GIS basic plans, so they have been operated on a legal basis and within an integrated framework. Moreover, as an integrated geospatial information system involves various institutions, the government has designated a specific organization for operating educational programs for locals while adopting the role of a mediator. KRIHS was responsible for providing education regarding the system for various actors, while its main role is establishing a strategic plan for the geospatial information system. Korea Land and Geospatial Informatix Corporation (LX) operates the National Land Information Education Center and the Spatial Data Academy to strengthen the capacity of professionals in the GIS-related field and people who are looking for jobs.

The Korean government has implemented several systematic educational programs to develop human resources, including a regional hub university program, specialized graduate schools, and online educational programs for geospatial data technologies (KRIHS, 2014d). The regional hub university programs have been conducted on objectives of enhancing government employees' capacity to fully take advantage of the geospatial data application system, training teachers in primary and secondary schools for better understanding the system to educate their students, and

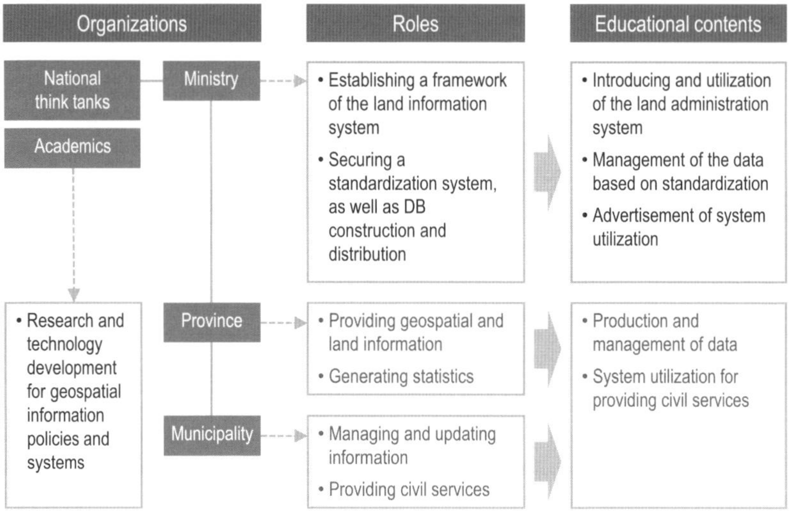

Figure 45. The roles of each organization and the customized education programs

promoting professionals in specific fields of industry and improve work performance.

According to the Spatial Data Industry Promotion Act, the specialized graduate school programs were implemented to train technical manpower specializing in geospatial data, thereby contributing to enhancing the country's technological competitiveness and promoting the development of relevant industries. The government supports the selected specialized graduate schools for five years to facilitate them to improve their competitiveness with long-term goals as well as specialization of their professional degree programs.

Moreover, the Korean government implemented online programs to attract a wide range of people interested in learning GIS to those who are compelled to learn GIS for their professions. Moreover, in-depth online programs have been conducted for government officials who took offline classes and are required to take intensified classes related to their tasks. Leveraging Korea's experiences, the developing countries may implement capacity-building programs for three tiers: governments, experts, and general citizens.

The government can run both short-term and long-term educational programs; the short ones are for occupational education to fully facilitate the established data system as well as advertising its applicability, and the long ones are for educating professionals who systemize and analyze the geospatial data. It is also critical to conduct the program for local governments in charge of collecting and managing the data in practice.

The development of human resources is a crucial task to foster geospatial industries. The public and private sectors can consider education programs in terms of three aspects: fostering specialized universities for geospatial data technologies and operating educational programs for industry-customized professionals and online programs, applying Korea's experiences. The government can also establish an authentication system for professionals in land value assessment, real estate transactions, and geospatial technologies.

The governments must promote programs for citizens to utilize the data system, protect the land tenure of the vulnerable group, and inform adequate ways of resolving land disputes and obtaining appropriate compensation. In the early stage of the development of the data system, the general public is not familiar with the system and the ways in which the system can be utilized. Therefore, it is crucial to advertise the advantages of the system for better awareness. Moreover, in developing countries, as numerous vulnerable populations suffer from land tenure insecurity, it is critical for the government to run programs for those who are not entirely aware of land laws and regulations that help them protect their own security. Moreover, the government can consider implementing consulting services for measures that ensure adequate compensation to protect their own rights.

INTERVIEW 6

Land conflict and resolution process in developing countries

In order to investigate the land conflict and resolution process of countries that have experienced situations that were similar to those under study, we conducted an interview with Jongjun Won, manager of the Business Strategy Planning Team, KOICA. He is an expert in charge of establishing and consulting KOICA's urban business strategy. The written interview was conducted on May 22, 2020, and the following contents were summarized and described.

The importance of the land system in developing countries

Readjustment of land systems must be prioritized in developing countries. Land-related issues do not have much social importance in general, as they are in the process of establishing overall political, economic, and social direction. However, a rational and transparent land system is a key task in the development of the national economy and the safety of the system. Moreover, it is necessary to push ahead with the readjustment of the land system at the stage of setting a large socioeconomic framework, given that the readjustment of the land system takes a long time because it has a direct stake in existing landuse customs and rights relations, as well as the lives of people.

Technical difficulties in adapting technologies

Almost all countries have a substantial understanding of the various systems being implemented in other countries, but the technical understanding for actual implementation is low. In Vietnam, the country with the highest growth rate in recent years and which has undergone similar development stages to the three countries, approximately 60 percent of all civil proceedings (as of 2015) were found to be related to land transactions. In the case of land compensation due to domestic financial investment and expansion of foreign direct investment, litigation appears to be high; in the process of taxation, there was a problem of tax equity related to land price calculation. To solve this problem, the Land Act was first enacted in 1987 after the economic reform of Doi Moi in 1986, including the granting of rights to landowners and the allocation of long-term land use rights in 1993; a revision to this was made once in 2003, and a large-scale revision was implemented in 2013 in the form of the New Land Act. In 2013, the new land law significantly added regulations on land use compared to the existing land law, and items in the 2003 revision also added provisions, which significantly increased the state's involvement in land use and management. This change can be seen as a result of social and economic inconvenience in the process of industrialization. Despite these efforts, information on land, housing, etc. held by central or local governments remains inaccurate due to unplanned urbanization. These governments mainly possess paper-type urban planning drawings that differ from the actual status.

ODA projects for land information and spatial information infrastructure

The international community's ODA focuses on building land information and spatial information infrastructure throughout the country rather than resolving land conflicts. Conflict management is dealt with in SDG16 – Peace, justice, and strong institutions – but it is difficult to recognize that there is a trend of cooperation in the international community because it becomes too detailed a subject when limited to the field of land. One of the efforts to resolve conflict is GIS, which is mainly used to support the construction of information systems such as land use management, system integration, urban web GIS, and housing and real estate management in developing countries. The goal is to support the resolution of conflicts caused by land ownership and transactions that frequently occur in developing countries by implementing projects to register and manage land information, such as land use management, cadastral management, land registration, and lease contract systems. By integrating and utilizing different types of data, we are attempting to establish a system that shortens the time of decision-making and work process for urban development, provides education and consulting, and supports sustainable urban development in developing countries. However, even in developed donor countries, GIS tends to be used as a means to achieve a specific purpose rather than as a business field. Korea's ODA is also attempting to respond to its limitations, but it is difficult to say that it is still focusing on inclusive growth and land conflict management.

Since it is only targeted at a few pilot areas, there are no actual results yet, but there is a continuous pursuit of projects for effectiveness. The practical use of land information at the national level requires the establishment of a unified database at the national level, not in only a few pilot areas. Next, there is a necessity of a system for continuous renewal of land information and the government's continued interest and policy for keeping up to date with the necessary budget, database and equipment, and the continued supply of professional personnel to cope with the various technical errors that may occur in the process. However, each agency that promotes the project has its own criteria and procedures for selecting the project, and there is a difference in recognition of different problems and priorities for the status of its partners. In addition, compared to projects that need to be promoted for many years, inter-agency projects cannot be efficiently linked due to unstable partner governance. Nevertheless, we are making continuous efforts to achieve effective results.

REFERENCES

Baek, Jong Cheon & Yun, Jeong Won. (1991). "A Study of the Korean War: Focused on the Results and Impacts." *Treatises on Korean History*, 28: 135-174. (백종천·윤정원. (1991). 「6·25전쟁에 대한 연구: 결과와 영향을 중심으로」. 『국사관논총』, 28: 135-174.)

Cho, Myeong Rae. (2004). "Gangnam as an Ark of the New Class." *Hwanghae Review*, 42: 25-40. (조명래. (2004). 「신상류층의 방주(方舟)로서의 강남」. 『황해문화』, 42: 25-40.)

Choi, Byung Sun. (2018). "Retrospect and Prospect of 40 Years of National Land Policy (III)." *Planning and Policy*, 443: 59-68. (최병선. (2018). 「국토정책 40년의 회고와 전망(III)」. 『국토연구원: 국토』, 443: 59-68.)

Choi, Dong Woon. (2014a). Determination of Facilities for the Residential Area Development Project for the Creation of the Resettlement Complex for Migrants in Seoul (23rd August 1972). Seoul Information Communication Plaza (website). (최동운. (2014a). 서울시 철거민 이주정착단지조성을 위한 일단의 주택지 조성사업 시설 결정(1972.08.23). 서울정보소통광장.) Available from: https://opengov.seoul.go.kr/seoul/1201643 [Accessed 18th February 2021].

Choi, Sang-Chul, Park, Se-Hoon, Lee, Hee-Jung, Jo, Ju-Hyun & Lee, Ju-Won. (2015). "A History of Urban Planning in Korea on the 70th Anniversary of Korea's Liberation Day." *Journal of Urban Information Service*, 401 (August): 3-32. (최상철·박세훈·이희정·조주현·이주원. (2015). 「광복 70주년 특집 우리나라 도시계획의 변천사」. 『도시정보』, 401: 3-32.)

Choi, Seong Hui. (2014b). "Urban Village and the History of Migration to City? A Case of Seoul Nowon-gu Joonggyebon-dong 104 Village." *The Journal of Next-Generation Humanities and Social Sciences*, 10(0): 163-178. (최성희. (2014b). 「도시 이주의 역사와 도시마을(Urban Village)? 서울 노원구(蘆原區) 중계본동(中溪本洞) 104(百四)마을」. 『차세대 인문사회연구』, 10(0): 163-178.)

Chung, Young-Iob. (2007). *Korea in the Fast Lane: Economic Development and Capital Formation*. Oxford, United Kingdom: Oxford University Press.

ECOS (Economic Statistics System). (2020). National Account: GDP and GNI by Economic Activity (website). (한국은행 경제통계시스템. (2020). 국민계정: 경제활동별 GDP 및 GNI.) Available from: https://ecos.bok.or.kr/flex/EasySearch.jsp [Accessed 3rd May 2020].

GIZ (Deutsche Gesellschaft für internationale Zusammenarbeit). (2017). *Understanding, Preventing Land Conflicts: A Practical Guide and Toolbox*. Bonn & Eschborn, Germany: GIZ.

Green Growth Committee of Korea. (2009). *Green Growth National Strategy and Five-*

Year Plan. Seoul, South Korea: Green Growth Committee. (녹색성장위원회. (2009).『녹색성장 국가전략 및 5개년 계획』. 서울, 대한민국: 녹색성장위원회.)

Heo, Soo-Yeol. (2012). "1945 Liberation and Economic Development of the Republic." *Journal of Korean Independence Movement Studies*, 43: 463-509. (허수열. (2012).「1945년 해방과 대한민국의 경제발전」.『한국독립운동사연구』, 43: 463-509.)

Hong, Sung-Eon. (2011). "A Study on Patterns of Cadastral Non-Coincidence and Methods for the Arrangement." *Journal of the National Geographic Society*, 45(3): 397-407. (홍성언. (2011).「지적불부합지의 유형별 조사와 정리 방법 연구」.『국토지리학회지』, 45(3): 397-407.)

HUFS (Hankuk University of Foreign Studies). (2013). *2012 Modularization of Korea's Development Experience: Land Reform in Korea*. Sejong, South Korea: KDI (Korea Development Institute) School of Public Policy and Management.

Jang, Bom. (2014). *The Present State of 104 Villages Ahead of Redevelopment*. Seoul, South Korea: SI. (장봄. (2014).『재개발을 앞둔 104마을의 현재』. 서울, 대한민국: 서울연구원.)

Jang, Se-Hoon. (1988). "Urbanization, Nationality and Urban Poor: Focused on the Seoul Metropolitan Government's Policy of Demolition and Maintenance of Unauthorized Settlements." *Korean Social History Association*, 14: 120-173. (장세훈. (1988).「도시화, 국가 그리고 도시 빈민-서울시의 무허가 정착지 철거 정비 정책을 중심으로」.『사회와 역사(구 한국사회사학회논문집)』, 14: 120-173.)

Joint Ministries of Korea. (2014). *2nd Green Growth Five-Year Plan (2014-2018)*. Seoul, South Korea: Green Growth Committee. (관계부처 합동. (2014).『제2차 녹색성장 5개년 계획(2014-2018)』. 서울, 대한민국: 녹색성장위원회.)

_____. (2019). *3rd Green Growth Five-Year Plan (2019-2023)*. Seoul, South Korea: Green Growth Committee. (관계부처 합동. (2019).『제3차 녹색성장 5개년 계획(2019-2023)』. 서울, 대한민국: 녹색성장위원회.)

Jun, Nam-Il, Kim, Myo-Jung, Yang, Se-Hwa, Hong, Hyung-Ock & Sohn, Sei-Kwan. (2007). "A Study on the Formation of Urban Squatter in Korea and Their Housing Culture from Socio-historical Point of View." *Journal of the Korean Housing Association*, 18(3): 9-18. (전남일·김묘정·양세화·홍형옥·손세관. (2007).「사회사적 관점에서 본 우리나라 도시빈민의 형성배경과 주거문화」.『한국주거학회논문집』, 18(3): 9-18.)

Jung, Hee Nam. (1994). "Accumulation, Legitimacy, Internationalization and the Role of Land Policies since Liberalization in 1945: The Retrospectives and Prospectives." *Proceedings of the Korean Association for Public Administration Conference*, December: 373-403. (정희남. (1994).「광복 후 한국 토지정책의 회고와 향후의 과제: 자본축적, 정치적 정당성, 세계화, 그리고 토지정책」.『한국행정학회 학술발표논문집』, 373-403.)

_____. (2010). "The Evolution of Korean Land Policies since Independence, 1948-2008." *Korea Real Estate Review*, 20(1): 281-306. (정희남. (2010).「정부수립 이후의 한국 토지정책 60년사 소고」.『부동산연구』, 20(1): 281-306.)

KEEI (Korea Energy Economics Institute). (2020). *Yearbook of Energy Statics*. Ulsan, South Korea: KEEI. (에너지경제연구원. (2020).『에너지통계연보』. 울산, 대한민국: 에너지경제연구원.)

KESS (Korean Educational Service). (2019). Brief Educational Statistics for 2019: School Entrance Rate. (교육통계서비스. (2019). 2019 간추린 교육통계: 진학률.) Available from: https://kess.kedi.re.kr/publ/publFile/pdfjs?survSeq=2019&menuSeq=3645&publSeq=3&menuCd=80211&itemCode=02&menuId=1_3&language [Accessed 22nd April 2020].

KFS (Korea Forest Service). (2013). *A Study on the Integrated Management of Landslide Hazardous Areas*. Daejeon, South Korea: KFS. (산림청. (2013). 『산사태 발생 위험지의 통합관리 방안 연구』. 대전, 대한민국: 산림청.)

_____. (2016). Forest Statics: Forest Area and Growing Stock (website). (산림청. (2016). e나라지표: 산림 면적 및 임목축적.) Available from: http://index.go.kr/potal/main/EachDtlPageDetail.do?idx_cd=1300 [Accessed 21st May 2020].

KICC (Korea Industrial Complex Corporation). (2020). Industrial Complex Status: The Number of Industrial Complex (website). (한국산업단지공단. (2020). 전국산업단지현황통계.) Available from: https://www.data.go.kr/data/3041272/fileData.do [Accessed 16th May 2020].

Kim, Do Hun. (2014). "Korea's Industrial Development and Future Challenges." *The Korean Economic Association*, 6(4): 15-35. (김도훈. (2014). 「한국 산업발전과 향후 과제」. 『한국경제학회』, 6(4): 15-35.)

Kim, Kwang-Joong. (2003). *Seoul, Twentieth Century: Growth & Change of the Last 100 Years*. Seoul, South Korea: SI.

_____, Lee, Injae, Jung, Sanghyuk & Jeon, Yookyung. (1996). *Housing Improvement Redevelopment History Study*. Seoul, South Korea: SI. (김광중·이인재·정상혁·전유경. (1996). 『주택개량재개발 연혁연구』. 서울, 대한민국: 서울연구원.)

Kim, Min Che. (1995). Encyclopedia of Korean Culture: Inflation (website). (김민채. (1995). 한국민족문화백과사전: 인플레이션.) Available from: http://encykorea.aks.ac.kr/Contents/Item/E0047119 [Accessed 5th May 2020].

Kim, Seon Woong. (2015). Land Readjustment Project. Seoul Solution (website). (김선웅. (2015). 서울주요정책: 토지구획정리사업.) Available from: https://seoulsolution.kr/ko [Accessed 17th April 2020].

Kim, Tae Oh & Choi, Mack Joong. (2018). "The Gwangju Mega Housing Complex Re-examined: Evolution into Self-sufficient New Town Based on Industrial Complex." *Journal of Korea Planning Association*, 53(4): 39-55. (김태오·최막중. (2018). 「광주대단지의 재조명: 공업단지에 의한 자족적 신도시로의 확장」. 『대한국토도시계획학회: 국토계획』, 53(4): 39-55.)

Kim, Young Ran. (2012). "Urban Water Circulation System Establishment Plan: The Effect of Urbanization on Water Circulation and the Current State of Seoul." *Water Journal*, 97: 27-31. (김영란. (2012). 「도시 물순환 체계 구축방안: 도시화가 물순환에 미치는 영향과 서울시 현황」. 『워터저널』, 97: 27-31.)

KLI (Korea Labor Institute). (2014). *A Study on Job Creation through Spatial Information Convergence*. Sejong, South Korea: KLI. (한국노동연구원. (2014). 『공간정보 융복합을 통한 일자리 창출 고용영향평가 연구』. 세종, 대한민국: 한국노동연구원.)

KNSIP (Korea National Spatial Data Infrastructure Portal). (2020). Green Belt (website). (국가공간정보포털. (2020). 개발제한구역지정관리/개발제한 구역.) Available from: http://data.nsdi.go.kr/dataset/15147 [Accessed 4th June 2020].

Korea University. (2014). *2014 Modularization of Korea's Development Experience: Experiences and Lessons of Green Growth.* Sejong, South Korea: KDI School of Public Policy and Management.

KOSIS (Korean Statistical Information Service), LH (Korea Land and Housing Corporation). (2020). Statistics of Urban Planning: Population Status in Urban Areas. (국가통계포털, 한국토지주택공사. (2020). 도시지역 인구현황.) Available from: https://kosis.kr/statHtml/statHtml.do?orgId=315&tblId=TX_315_2009_H1001&vw_cd=MT_ZTITLE&list_id=315_31502_008&seqNo=&lang_mode=ko&language=kor&obj_var_id=&itm_id=&conn_path=MT_ZTITLE [Accessed 20th May 2020].

KOSIS, MOLIT (Ministry of Land, Infrastructure and Transport). (2020). Road Status: Road Status by City and Province. (국가통계포털, 국토교통부. (2020). 시도별 도로 보급률.) Available from: https://kosis.kr/statHtml/statHtml.do?orgId=116&tblId=DT_MLTM_966&vw_cd=MT_ZTITLE&list_id=M2_10&seqNo=&lang_mode=ko&language=kor&obj_var_id=&itm_id=&conn_path=MT_ZTITLE [Accessed 7th May 2020].

KOSIS, Statistics Korea. (1953a). Korea Statistical Yearbook: Demolition of the Erosion Control Facilities. (국가통계포털, 통계청. (1953a). 한국통계연감: 사방시설 피해.) Available from: http://kosis.kr/statHtml/statHtml.do?orgId=999S&tblId=DT_999S_151053&conn_path=I3 [Accessed 5th June 2020].

_____. (1953b). Korea Statistical Yearbook: Demolition of the Water Supply Facilities. (국가통계포털, 통계청. (1953b). 한국통계연감: 수도시설 피해.) Available from: http://kosis.kr/statHtml/statHtml.do?orgId=999S&tblId=DT_999S_150053&conn_path=I3 [Accessed 5th June 2020].

_____. (1953c). Korea Statistical Yearbook: Roads Demolition. (국가통계포털, 통계청. (1953c). 한국통계연감: 도로 총피해.) Available from: http://kosis.kr/statHtml/statHtml.do?orgId=999S&tblId=DT_999S_147053&conn_path=I3 [Accessed 5th June 2020].

_____. (2010). Korea Statistical Yearbook: Housing Demolition. (국가통계포털, 통계청. (2010). 한국통계연감: 주택 피해.) Available from: http://kosis.kr/statHtml/statHtml.do?orgId=999S&tblId=DT_999S_134053&conn_path=I3 [Accessed 28th May 2020].

_____. (2019). Future Population Estimation: Major Demographic Indicators (Population Growth Rate). (국가통계포털, 통계청. (2019). 인구증가추세: 주요 인구지표(성비, 인구성장률, 인구구조, 부양비 등).) Available from: https://kosis.kr/statHtml/statHtml.do?orgId=101&tblId=DT_1BPB002&conn_path=I3 [Accessed 24th February 2021].

_____. (2021a). Economically Active Population Survey: Unemployment Rate by Gender/Age Group. (국가통계포털, 통계청. (2021a). 성/연령별 실업률.) Available from: https://kosis.kr/statHtml/statHtml.do?orgId=101&tblId=DT_1DA7102S&conn_path=I3 [Accessed 24th February 2021].

_____. (2021b). National Business Survey: Number of Establishments and Workers by Region (City, Gun, Gu), Industry and Establishment Size. (국가통계포털, 통계청. (2021b). 시도·산업·사업체구분별 사업체 수, 종사자 수.) Available from: https://

kosis.kr/statHtml/statHtml.do?orgId = 101&tblId = DT_1K52C01&conn_path = I3 [Accessed 24th February 2021].

KOSIS, UN (United Nations). (2018). International Statistical Yearbook: Urbanization Rate. (국가통계포털, UN. (2018). 국제통계연감: 도시화율.) Available from: https://kosis.kr/statHtml/statHtml.do?orgId = 101&tblId = DT_2KAA204&vw_cd = MT_RTITLE&list_id = 101_001_A&seqNo = &lang_mode = ko&language = kor&obj_var_id = &itm_id = &conn_path = MT_RTITLE [Accessed 10th May 2020].

KRIHS (Korea Research Institute for Human Settlements). (1995). *A Study on the Measures to Promote the Land Lease System in Korea*. Sejong, South Korea: KRIHS. (국토연구원. (1995). 『토지임대차 활성화방안』. 세종, 대한민국: 국토연구원.)

_____. (2006). *Land Policy Direction and Implementation Strategy Preparing for the Advanced Society (I)*. Sejong, South Korea: KRIHS. (국토연구원. (2006). 『선진사회를 향한 토지정책 방향 및 추진전략 연구(I)』. 세종, 대한민국: 국토연구원.)

_____. (2007). *Establishment of National GIS of Korea*. KRIHS Special Report Vol. 8. Sejong, South Korea: KRIHS.

_____. (2010). *Reestablishment of Land Policy to Paradigm Shift*. Sejong, South Korea: MOLIT. (국토연구원. (2010). 『토지정책 패러다임 재정립 방안 연구』. 세종, 대한민국: 국토교통부.)

_____. (2012). *2011 Modularization of Korea's Development Experience: Policy for the Construction and Supply of Affordable Housing in Korea*. Sejong, South Korea: KDI School of Public Policy and Management.

_____. (2014a). *2013 Modularization of Korea's Development Experience: The Establishment of Korea Land Information System (KLIS)*. Sejong, South Korea: KDI School of Public Policy and Management.

_____. (2014b). *2013 Modularization of Korea's Development Experience: The Expropriation and Compensation System in Korea*. Sejong, South Korea: KDI School of Public Policy and Management.

_____. (2014c). *Korea Land Information System (KLIS)*. Sejong, South Korea: KRIHS.

_____. (2014d). *Geospatial Human Resource Development*. Sejong, South Korea: KRIHS.

_____. (2014e). *Korea Planning Support System (KOPSS)*. Sejong, South Korea: KRIHS. (국토연구원. (2014e). 『국토공간계획지원체계(KOPSS)』. 세종, 대한민국: 국토연구원.)

Kwon, Rak Yong. (2012). "The Conflict Composition among Classify Subjects in Gwangju Grand Housing Complex Construction: Focused on an Existing Urban District of Seongnam." Master dissertation. Department of Civil and Environmental Engineering College of Engineering. Seoul National University. (권락용. (2012). 「광주대단지 사업의 주체별 갈등구성: 성남 본시가지를 중심으로」. 서울대학교 건설환경공학부 석사학위 논문.)

Lee, Chang Moo, Ahn, Chang Nam & Kim, Ji Yeon. (2014). *2014 Modularization of Korea's Development Experience: Enhancing Transparency in Real Estate Ownership and Transaction: Cases of Two Policy Reforms in Korea*. Sejong, South Korea: KDI School of Public Policy and Management.

Lee, Ho Jun. (2015). "Problems of the Existing Public Expropriation System and the Improvement Plan." *Real Estate Focus*, 85: 65-73. (이호준. (2015). 「현행 공용수용제도의 문제점과 개선방안」. 『부동산 포커스』, 85: 65-73.)

Lee, Ji Hye. (2009). Balance of Trade and Payments. KDI Economic Information Center (Website). (이지혜. (2009). 무역수지와 국제수지.) Available from: https://eiec.kdi.re.kr/material/clickView.do?click_yymm=201512&cidx=1108 [Accessed 22nd April 2020].

Lee, Shin. (2014). Seoul Transport Operation and Information Services (TOPIS). Seoul Solution (website). (이신. (2014). 서울교통정보센터(TOPIS).) Available from: https://seoulsolution.kr/ko/content/652 [Accessed 20th April 2020].

Lim, Miri. (2012). "A Study on Reappraising a Result of the Gwangju Housing Complex Event in 1971." *Journal of Memory and Vision*, 26: 228-268. (임미리. (2012).「1971년 광주대단지 사건의 재해석」.『기억과 전망』, 26: 228-268.)

LX (Korea Land and Geospatial Informatix Corporation). (2011). *Preparation of the Land and Tenure Security Program in Haiti*. Seoul, South Korea: Korea EximBank.

Ministry of Environment. (2014). *The Natural Environment of the Country as Seen by Statistics*. Sejong, South Korea: Ministry of Environment. (환경부. (2014).『통계로 본 국토·자연환경』. 세종, 대한민국: 환경부.)

MOLIT (Ministry of Land, Infrastructure and Transport). (2011). *Development Restriction Area 1971-2011*. Sejong, South Korea: MOLIT. (국토교통부. (2011).『개발제한구역 40년: 1971-2011』. 세종, 대한민국: 국토교통부.)

______. (2018a). *6th National Geographic Information System Basic Plan (2018-2022)*. Sejong, South Korea: MOLIT. (국토교통부. (2018a).『제6차 국가공간정보정책 기본계획(2018-2022)』. 세종, 대한민국: 국토교통부.)

______. (2018b). Professional Training Plan for Public Officials in Charge of Cadastral and Spatial Information of Local Governments in 2018. MOLIT Advance Public Information Bulletin Board (website). (국토교통부. (2018b). 2018년 지자체 지적·공간정보 담당공무원 전담교육 계획. 국토교통부 사전공표정보게시판.) Available from: http://www.molit.go.kr/USR/BORD0201/m_34879/DTL.jsp?id=www_info&cate=&mode=view&idx=30381&key=&search=&search_regdate_s=2018-01-15&search_regdate_e=2019-01-15&order=&desc=asc&srch_prc_stts=&item_num=0&search_dept_id=&search_dept_nm=&srch_usr_nm=N&srch_usr_titl=N&srch_usr_ctnt=N&srch_mng_nm=N&old_dept_nm=&search_gbn=&search_section=&source=&search1=&lcmspage=6 [Accessed 18th February 2021].

______. (2019). *Annual Report on National Land Planning and Utilization 2019*. Sejong, South Korea: MOLIT. (국토교통부. (2019).『국토의 계획 및 이용에 관한 연차보고서』. 세종, 대한민국: 국토교통부.)

______. (2020). Real Transaction Price Disclosure System. MOLIT (website). (국토교통부. (2020). 실거래가 공개시스템.) Available from: http://rtdown.molit.go.kr/ [Accessed 18th May 2020].

______. (2021). Geospatial Information Industry Sales Exceeded 9 Trillion Won. Press Release of MOLIT (website). (국토교통부. (2021). 공간정보산업 매출액 9조 돌파. 국토교통부 보도자료.) Available from: https://www.molit.go.kr/USR/NEWS/m_71/dtl.jsp?lcmspage=1&id=95085029 [Accessed 18th February 2021].

Nam, Gi Up & Lee, Jin Su. (2020). "2019 Land Analysis of Land Ownership Status: How Unequal is Ownership?" *Land and Liberty Report*, 17. (남기업·이진수.

(2020).「2019 토지 소유는 얼마나 불평등한가?」.『토지자유리포트』, 17.)

National Archives of Korea. (2021). Photo Archives of Korean War: Ruins in Seoul (website). (국가기록원. (2021). 6·25전쟁 사진 자료실: 서울의 폐허.) Available from: https://theme.archives.go.kr/next/625/viewMain.do [Accessed 18th February 2021].

National Geographic Information Service. (2020). National Territory Information Platform: National Statistical Map. (국토지리정보원. (2020). 국토정보플랫폼: 국토통계지도.) Available from: http://map.ngii.go.kr/mn/mainPage.do [Accessed 12th June 2020].

NGII (National Geographic Information Institute). (2018). *The National Atlas of Korea (III)*. Seoul, South Korea: Jinhanbook. (국토지리정보원. (2018).『대한민국 국가지도집(III)』. 서울, 대한민국: 진한엠앤비.)

_____. (2021). National Territory Information Platform: NGII (Website). (국토지리정보원. (2021). 국토정보플랫폼: 국토지리정보원.) Available from: https://www.ngii.go.kr/kor/content.do?sq=237 [Accessed 18th February 2021].

NIFS (National Institute of Forest Science). (2014). *2013 Modularization of Korea's Development Experience: Forest Resource Development in Korea*. Sejong, South Korea: KDI School of Public Policy and Management.

OECD (Organization for Economic Cooperation and Development). (2016). Green Growth Indicators: Patents on Environment Technologies Data (2016). Available from: https://data.oecd.org/envpolicy/patents-on-environment-technologies.htm [Accessed 1st June 2020].

_____. (2019). Income Inequality Data (2015-2019). Available from: https://data.oecd.org/inequality/income-inequality.htm [Accessed 1st June 2020].

_____. (2020a). Education at a Glance: Population Data with Tertiary Education. Available from: https://data.oecd.org/eduatt/population-with-tertiary-education.htm [Accessed 2nd June 2020].

_____. (2020b). Environment at a Glance: Municipal Waste Data. Available from: https://data.oecd.org/waste/municipal-waste.htm [Accessed 2nd June 2020].

_____. (2020c). Environment at a Glance: Air and GHG Emissions Data. Available from: https://data.oecd.org/air/air-and-ghg-emissions.htm [Accessed 2nd June 2020].

_____. (2020d). OECD Economic Outlook: Gross Domestic Product (GDP) Data. Available from: https://data.oecd.org/gdp/gross-domestic-product-gdp.htm [Accessed 2nd June 2020].

Onbid (Online Bidding). (2014). KEPCO (Korea Electric Power Corporation) Building Bid Price. (온비드. (2014). 한국전력빌딩 감정평가정보.) Available from: https://www.onbid.co.kr/op/cta/cltrdtl/collateralRealEstateDetail.do?cltrHstrNo=2084872&cltrNo=952391&plnmNo=299051&pbctNo=334307&scrnGrpCd=0001&pbctCdtnNo=2161872 [Accessed 21st March 2021].

Park, Myeong-Ho. (2015). "Land Reform and Its Impact on Farmers' Living Standard." *Korean Society for Comparative Economics*, 22(2): 1-36. (박명호. (2015).「한국 농지개혁의 파급효과: 농민생활을 중심으로」.『한국비교경제학회』, 22(2): 1-36.)

PCBND (Presidential Committee for Balanced National Development). (2021). Committee Functions and Organization. PCBND (website). (국가균형발전위원회.

(2021). 위원회 기능 및 조직.) Available from: http://www.balance.go.kr/base/contents/view?contentsNo=26&menuLevel=2&menuNo=30 [Accessed 18th February 2021].

Ryu, Sang Yun. (2017). "The Allocation of Foreign Aids among Korean Firms in 1954." *The Review of Business History (KABH)*, 32(3): 5-23. (류상윤. (2017). 「경제부흥원조의 시작과 기업의 대응」. 『경영사연구』, 32(3): 5-23.)

Seo, Chan Su. (1987). "The Process of Human Capital Accumulation in Korea and Its Factors." *The Korean National Economic Association*, 5: 69-90. (서찬수. (1987). 「한국의 인적자본축정과정과 그 요인」. 『한국경제통상학회』, 5: 69-90.)

Seo, Jung Seok. (2013). *Contemporary History of Korea Reviewing with Pictures*. Paju, South Korea: WoongJinbooks. (서중석. (2013). 『사진과 그림으로 보는 한국 현대사』. 파주, 대한민국: 웅진지식하우스.)

Seo, Soon Tak. (2000). "The Status and Countermeasures of Reckless Development in Quasi-Agricultural and Forestry Areas." *Journal of Planning and Policy*, 226 (August): 6-17. (서순탁. (2000). 「수도권 준농림지역 난개발 실태와 대책」. 『국토연구원: 국토』, 226: 6-17.)

Seoul Metropolitan Archives. (2018). Photo Archives of Flood District of Cheonggyecheon (26th August 1967). Seoul Metropolitan Archives (website). (서울기록원. (2018). 청계천 수해지구의 사진(1967.08.26.).) Available form: https://archives.seoul.go.kr/item/6643 [Accessed 4th May 2020].

Seoul Metropolitan Government. (1989). Land Readjustment Project Status. Seoul Metropolitan Government Land Readjustment (website). (서울시. (1989). 토지구획 사업현황.) Available from: http://115.84.165.78/user/intro02.do?leftMenu=1 [Accessed 17th May 2020].

_____. (2012). *104 Village Preservation Plan (2012)*. Seoul, South Korea: Seoul Metropolitan Government. (서울시. (2012). 『백사마을 보존계획안(2012)』. 서울, 대한민국: 서울시.)

_____. (2017a). *Academic Service for Monitoring the Ecological Environment of the Umyeon Mountain Landslide Recovery Site and Surrounding Areas*. Seoul, South Korea: Seoul Metropolitan Government. (서울시. (2017a). 『우면산 산사태 복구지와 주변지역 생태환경 모니터링 학술용역』. 서울, 대한민국: 서울시.)

_____. (2017b). *White Paper of Seoul Land Readjustment Project (I)*. Seoul, South Korea: Seoul Metropolitan Government. (서울시. (2017b). 『서울 토지구획정리사업 백서(상권)』. 서울, 대한민국: 서울시.)

_____. (2020). Project Implementation Status: Korea Housing Corporation, Hwagok District. Seoul Metropolitan Government Land Readjustment (website). (서울시. (2020). 사업시행현황: 대한주택공사시행지(화곡지구).) Available from: http://115.84.165.78/user/wtp.do?leftMenu=4 [Accessed 17th May 2020].

_____. (2021a). 3D Seoul Map. Smart Seoul Map Portal (website). (서울시. (2021a). 3D 지도. 스마트서울포탈.) Available from: https://map.seoul.go.kr/smgis2/ [Accessed 15th February 2021].

_____. (2021b). Virtual Seoul Based on 3D. Smart Seoul Portal (website). (서울시. (2021b). 3D 기반 Virtual Seoul 구축. 스마트서울포탈.) Available from: https://smart.seoul.go.kr/board/25/70/board_view.do?&listType=list&bcstIdx1=

43&bdOpenYn=Y [Accessed 18th February 2021].

Seoul Metropolitan Urban Planning Bureau. (2016). Seoul Metropolitan Urban Planning Terminology Dictionary: Replotting. Naver Encyclopedia of Knowledge (website). (서울시 도시계획국. (2016). 서울시 도시계획 용어사전: 환지. 네이버지식백과사전.) Available from: https://terms.naver.com/entry.naver?docId=6079223&cid=67350&categoryId=67350 [Accessed 24th February 2021].

Seoul Museum of History. (2012). *104 Village: Joonggyebon-dong 104*. Seoul, South Korea: Seoul Museum of History. (서울역사박물관. (2012). 『104마을: 중계본동 산 104번지』. 서울, 대한민국: 서울역사박물관.)

Seoul Open Data Plaza. (2019). Data on the Status of Existing Unlicensed Buildings in Seoul (website). (서울열린데이터광장. (2019). 서울시 기존 무허가건축물현황.) Available from: http://data.seoul.go.kr/dataList/OA-15595/F/1/datasetView.do [Accessed 22nd February 2021].

Seoul Real Estate Information Plaza. (2021). Real Estate Comprehensive Information: Land Use Plan (website). (서울부동산정보광장. (2021). 부동산 종합정보: 토지이용계획.) Available from: https://land.seoul.go.kr:444/land/wskras/generalInfo.do# [Accessed 13th February 2021].

Seoul TOPIS. (2020). Urban Management Using Urban Spatial Data. Seoul Topis (website). (서울시 교통정보 시스템. (2020). 도시공간데이터를 활용한 도시관리.) Available from: https://topis.seoul.go.kr/ [Accessed 22nd May 2020].

SI (The Seoul Institute). (2014). *Seoul Statistical Series (I): Seoul Population Based on Statistics*. Seoul, South Korea: SI. (서울연구원. (2014). 『서울통계연구(I): 통계로 본 서울인구』. 서울, 대한민국: 서울연구원.)

______. (2020) *Changing Profile of Seoul (III)*. Seoul, South Korea: SI. (서울연구원. (2020). 『지표로 본 서울 변천(III)』. 서울, 대한민국: 서울연구원.)

SMFMC (Seoul Metropolitan Facilities Management Corporation). (2020). General Status of Traffic Information Office (January 2020). SMFMC (website). (서울시설공단. (2020). 교통정보처 종합현황(2020.01.).) Available from: https://www.sisul.or.kr/open_content/main/bbs/bbsMsgDetail.do?msg_seq=1215&bcd=branchbiz [Accessed 18th February 2021].

Son, Jeong-Mok. (2003). "50 Years of Urban History: Gwangju New Town Incident." *Urban Issues*, 38(420): 89-109. (손정목. (2003). 「도시 50년사: 광주대단지 사건」. 『도시문제』, 38(420): 89-109.)

______. (2005). *Story of 60 Years in Korean Cities Series (I)*. Paju, South Korea: Hanul. (손정목. (2005) 『한국 도시 60년의 이야기(I)』. 파주, 대한민국: 한울.)

Soumitra, Dutta, Bruno, Lanvin & Sacha, Wunsch-Vicent. (2019). *Global Innovation Index 2019: Creating Healthy Lives-The Future of Medical Innovation*. Geneva, Switzerland: WIPO (World Intellectual Property Organization).

The Economic Statistics Department of Bank of Korea. (2005). *60 Years of Liberation in Figures*. Seoul, South Korea: Bank of Korea. (한국은행 경제통계국. (2005). 『숫자로 보는 광복 60년』. 서울, 대한민국: 한국은행)

The Right Land. (2020a). Cases of Cadastral Resurvey Project. The Right Land (website). (바른땅. (2020a). 기대효과: 지적재조사 사례.) Available from: https://www.newjijuk.go.kr/promote/case.do [Accessed 11th June 2020].

______. (2020b). Introduction of Cadastral Resurvey Project. The Right Land (website). (바른땅. (2020b). 지적재조사 소개.) Available from: https://www.newjijuk.go.kr/promote/why.do [Accessed 7th June 2020].

______. (2021). Procedure: How Is the Cadastral Resurvey Project Done? The Right Land (website). (바른땅. (2021). 추진절차: 지적재조사는 어떻게 이루어지나요?) Available from: https://www.newjijuk.go.kr/promote/how.do [Accessed 20th February 2021].

The Seoul Research Data Service. (2000). Photo of Guro Industrial Complex. Seoul 2000 Urban Form and Landscape, Seoul Metropolitan Government (website). (서울연구데이터서비스. (2000). 사진으로 본 서울: 구로산업단지.) Available from: http://data.si.re.kr/psearch?keys=%EA%B5%AC%EB%A1%9C%EA%B3%B5%EB%8B%A8&or=&phrase=&negative= [Accessed 22nd April 2020].

______. (2015). Photo of the Ttukseom Han River Park. Seoul 2015 Urban Form and Landscape, Seoul Metropolitan Government (website). (서울연구데이터서비스. (2015). 사진으로 본 서울: 뚝섬한강공원.) Available from: http://data.si.re.kr/psearch?keys=%EB%9A%9D%EC%84%AC%ED%95%9C%EA%B0%95&or=&phrase=& negative= [Accessed 22nd April 2020].

UNDP (United Nations Development Programme). (2019). Human Development Reports: Human Development Data (1990-2018). UNDP (website). Available from: http://hdr.undp.org/en/data [Accessed 2nd May 2020].

United Nations, Department of Economic and Social Affairs. (2018). World Urbanization Prospects: The 2018 Revision, Online Edition. Available from: https://population.un.org/wup/Download/ [Accessed 28th May 2020].

USAID (United States Agency for International Development). (2013). Land and Conflict: Land Disputes and Land Conflicts. USAID (blog). Available from: https://www.land-links.org/issue-brief/land-disputes-and-land-conflict/ [Accessed 12th April 2020].

WBG (The World Bank Group). (2014). CO_2 Emissions (Kt). Available from: https://data.worldbank.org/indicator/EN.ATM.CO2E.KT [Accessed 18th April 2020].

______. (2015). *How Innovations in Land Administration Reform Improve on Doing Business*. Washington, DC, USA: WBG.

______. (2019). *WBG Group Strategy for Fragility, Conflict, and Violence (FCV) 2020-2025: Draft for Consultation*. Washington, DC, USA: WBG.

______. (2020). World Bank Open Data: GDP (Current US$) (1960-2018). Available from: https://data.worldbank.org/indicator/NY.GDP.MKTP.CD [Accessed 18th April 2020].

Wehrmann, Babette. (2006). *Landkonflikte im Urbanen und Peri-urbanen Raum von Großstädten in Entwicklungsländern: Mit Beispielen aus Accra und Phnom Penh*. Berlin, Germany: LIT.

Republic of Korea Armed Forces. (2010). Photo of Seoul during the Korean War. *Defense Photo Magazine*. (대한민국 국군. (2010). 6·25전쟁 당시 서울 모습. 『국방화보』.) Available from: https://www.flickr.com/photos/kormnd/albums/72157630292490846/with/7445971428/ [Accessed 30th September 2021].

INDEX

Principal investigator

Saehoon Kim is Associate Professor at Seoul National University Graduate School of Environmental Studies. He graduated from the Architecture Department at SNU and Harvard GSD. He is co-running the Urban Studies and Design Lab and authored a book titled *Exploring the City through Cities* (2017).

Researchers

Jihun Mun is a Ph.D. student in the Interdisciplinary Program in Landscape Architecture, Seoul National University Graduate School of Environmental Studies. He graduated from the Architecture Department at Inha University and Interdisciplinary Program in Urban Design at SNU.

Gukhwa Jang is a Ph.D. student in the Interdisciplinary Program in Landscape Architecture and Integrated Major in Smart City Global Convergence, Seoul National University Graduate School of Environmental Studies. She graduated from the Landscape Architecture Department at Kyungpook National University and earned a master's degree from GSES at SNU.

Sehyung Won is working as an urban development specialist at the Seoul Urban Solutions Agency of the Seoul Housing & Communities Corporation. After graduating from the Architecture Department at Inha University, he studied urban planning and design at Seoul National University Graduate School of Environmental Studies. He lectured on urban design theory at the Korea National University of Transportation.

Young Eun Kim is a Ph.D. student in the Interdisciplinary Program in Landscape Architecture and Integrated Major in Smart City Global Convergence, Seoul National University Graduate School of Environmental Studies. She graduated from the Architecture Department at Kyung Hee University and earned a master's degree from GSES at SNU.

Hayoung Kim is a Ph.D. student in the Interdisciplinary Program in Urban Design, Seoul National University. She graduated from the Architecture Department at Hanyang University and Interdisciplinary Program in Urban Design at SNU.

Kyung-in Choi is a Ph.D. student in the Interdisciplinary Program in Landscape Architecture, Seoul National University Graduate School of Environmental Studies. She graduated from the Architecture Department at Ewha Womans University and Interdisciplinary Program in Urban Design at SNU.

So Young Lee is a Ph.D. student in the Interdisciplinary Program in Urban Design, Seoul National University. She graduated from the Architecture Department at Ewha Womans University and Architecture Department at SNU.